KU-314-849

EUROPA MINOR

By the same author

Travel

GRAND TOUR*
LORDS OF THE EQUATOR*
THE ORPHANED REALM*
WITHIN THE TAURUS
(*A Journey in Asiatic Turkey*)

Fiction

THE RUTHLESS INNOCENT*

General

SOCIETY RACKET*
THE CENTURY OF THE COMMON PEER

* *Writing as Patrick Balfour*

LORD KINROSS

EUROPA MINOR

Journeys in Coastal Turkey

THE TRAVEL BOOK CLUB
121 CHARING CROSS ROAD
LONDON W.C.2

Printed in Great Britain by
Butler & Tanner Ltd., Frome and London

To
AMY and WALTER SMART

CONTENTS

Contents

PREFACE

THE PLATEAU OF ANATOLIA, within the encircling barrier of the Taurus, is essentially Asia Minor, geographically an outpost of Asia. Its coastal lands 'without the Taurus', whose formative influences have come largely from the West, are rather 'Europa Minor', geographically a fourth shore of Europe. I have presumed so to define them in the title of this book, a companion volume to *Within the Taurus*. It is a title incidentally which, in the political sense, might well be applied to modern Turkey as a whole. For the Turkish Republic, built by Atatürk on western foundations, is gradually developing, like Greece its neighbour, into an integral part of Europe.

The book deals, not with a single journey, but with a series of journeys, made between 1947 and 1954, ranging from Antioch and the Syrian frontier in the South-east to Adrianople and the Greek frontier in the North-west, covering the greater part of the 'Turkish Riviera' which fringes the Mediterranean and Aegean Seas.

My thanks are due to the Turkish Press, Broadcasting and Tourist Department, in Ankara, for many facilities on these journeys, and for the majority of the photographs which illustrate the book; to Mr. David Balfour, lately British Consul-General in Izmir, and Mrs. Balfour, whose hospitality, there and on board the motor yacht *Elfin*, enabled much of it to be written; to Mr. and Mrs. Seton Lloyd, of the British Institute of Archaeology in Ankara; Dr. Paul Underwood, of the museum of St. Sophia, in Istanbul; Mr. T. J. P. Tedesco, late of the British Consulate-General in Iskenderun; Mr. R. E. Wilkinson, of the British Consulate-General in Izmir; Mr. C. J. A. Bolton, late of the British Consulate in Mersin, and Mrs. Bolton; Mr. T. Millington, O.B.E., of the War Graves Commission, Çanakkale—all for much hospitality, assistance and information ; to Mrs. Nermin Streater and Mr. C. E. Stevens for help with the proofs ; and above all to the Turkish authorities, throughout the country, for their continual courtesy and help.

Finally I must thank Vice-Admiral Sir John A. Edgell, K.B.E., C.B., for permission to use extracts from the unpublished diary of Commander H. E. Edgell, R.N., written in 1845, and to Mr. Bernard Ashmole, Keeper of Greek and Roman Antiquities in the British Museum, for help in this connection.

CHAPTER I

ANTIOCH AND CILICIA

To the Mediterranean—'A lot of old pots'—The Syrian Frontier—Antioch and Antakya—Daphne yesterday and today—The Cotton City of Adana—Peoples of the Coast—Mersin

SUDDENLY the Mediterranean lay spread beneath me, shining in welcome, stretching away towards Europe. It promised relief from the eternal plateau, Asiatic and stern behind the parapets of the Taurus, and the ungrateful plains beneath them.As I drove down over the pass the slopes around me were alive with olives, alight with pines. Windows in the villages winked in the sunlight, rivulets sparkled as they danced away down to the sea.

At a café with a fountain I paused to wash off the dust of the plateau and refresh myself with a glass of *raki*. It was served to me, with discouraging discretion, out of sight of the road. The road at last was of tarmac, American cars spiralling around its bends with a Levantine shrieking of brakes. Presently a new damp heat seeped up to envelop me, and the port of Iskenderun emerged below, from steaming gardens of bougainvillea and eucalyptus and palm. The sea, alas, was imprisoned, in sultry stagnation, within the landlocked shelter of the Alexandrine Gulf of Issus.

The port, moreover, lacked life. Its Turkish inhabitants sat stodgily along an uncompleted sea-front. Two ramshackle 'casinos' leant out over the water on rough precarious piles. But there was red mullet to eat—and more *raki*. Moreover the hotel was new, and for the moment living up to its newness. After the inns of the plateau it seemed almost luxurious. A young Turkish schoolmaster, fresh from Istanbul and with a good command of English, talked to me in the doorway as I was taking what air there was, after dinner. He fetched from his room a few antiquities, Hellenistic in style, which he had unearthed on sites nearby—a statuette, a dish, the fragment of a vase.

'Please take them,' he said. 'There are many more where I found them.'

I declined politely: they would hardly survive the rigours of Turkish bus travel.

Each weekend, he said, he went digging. He had shown the sites to the authorities, only to be rebuffed by the answer:

'Who cares about a lot of old pots?'

* * *

So much for the age of Alexander. Once this was his city—Alexandria ad Issum, Alexandretta, Iskenderun—founded to mark his victory in that crucial conflict of history, the Battle of Issus. On this battlefield, some twenty miles north, he defeated the Persians, finally turning the tide from the East which the Greeks had checked at Salamis and Plataea, and reminding Darius accordingly: 'Your ancestors invaded Macedonia and the rest of Greece. I crossed over into Asia for the purpose of avenging these wrongs . . . for the future, whenever thou sendest, send to me as to the Great King of Asia.'[1] The Middle East lay at his feet. Thenceforward for nearly a thousand years, a Hellenic civilization prevailed over its lands.

Already for centuries it had prevailed, to a more limited extent, over its coasts. Here, differing profoundly from the landsmen, were colonies of sea-faring peoples, not only Greeks but Phoenicians, races of an expansive, questing nature. When the tide turned back, and successive waves of Arabs and Turks swamped the debatable lands once more, the Greeks and the Syrians—Semitic successors of the Phoenicians—remained on the coasts. The Turks are men of the plateau, withdrawn and dour, administrators by nature, and soldiers. Sensibly enough, they left their trade to the seamen, whose colonies—political no longer, commercial still—continued to flourish. It was only a generation ago, with the birth of a new Turkey, that the Greeks were finally driven away—victims of twentieth-century nationalism.

And now here by the sea, sitting silently among a lot of old pots. were the Turks—the men of the plateau. Sallow in complexion, slow in rhythm, they struck an un-Mediterranean note.

* * *

The sea having belied its initial welcome, I was glad next day to be greeted by the Acting British Consul-General, a Maltese with all the

[1] Quoted by J. B. Bury. *A History of Greece*. London: 1912.

effusive good fellowship of his kind, who drove me back up the mountainside to rest for a night or so in a châlet amid woods of scented Aleppo pine. Beneath us was the road to Aleppo itself. For nearby were Ptolemy's 'Syrian Gates', the natural highway from the coast up over the Amanus to the Syrian plateau. Atatürk had barred them in the name of strategy and self-determination, through his one and only land grab, the occupation in 1939 of the Sanjak of Alexandretta, then under French mandate. Now Iskenderun looked the other way. A new strategic highway led up over the Taurus and across the Anatolian plateau to Erzurum, while American engineers were enlarging the port to feed this potential Eastern front. Our châlet was the summer residence of an Armenian doctor, a Syrian subject living in Aleppo, who no longer had access to it.

Meanwhile, along their artificial frontiers, Turks and Syrians thrived on a number of intricate contraband operations, involving, among other commodities, pistachio nuts and dollars. The smugglers, who were periodically imprisoned, were the agents of rich merchants, who got off scot-free. The Consul entertained me with such Levantine gossip, and with shrewd observations on the Turkish character. In Ottoman times he would have been a Greek, like the Consul in Mersin who similarly entertained Davis.[1] 'Now,' he had deplored, of the Turks, 'they are beginning to open their eyes a good deal more, and it is not so easy to manage them. . . . Would to God they would all disappear!'

My host, who expressed no such drastic sentiments, drove me to Antioch, the great capital built by Seleucus in the name of his master, the dead Alexander. Beneath a castle on a peak, a relic of the Crusaders, the road ran straight as a ribbon across the plain, between ranks of flowering oleanders and poplars—a relic, Roman in character, of the short-lived French occupation. He left me at the *Turism Oteli*, where I suffered at nights from a naked light, blazing into my room from the hallway. From two bewildered small boys, who seemed after dark to be in sole charge of the hotel, I gathered that it could be extinguished only at some distant main, together with all the lights of the town.

Antioch, as it happens, was remarkable for its street-lamps even in classical times—lamps, taking the place of the sun, 'which leave the Egyptian festival of illumination far behind; and with us night is

[1] E. J. Davis. *Life in Asiatic Turkey*. London: 1879.

distinguished from day only by the difference of lighting.'[1] When Seleucus planned the city, on the fashionable grid plan, he is said to have stationed elephants at the corners of the site, where towers were to be built, and to have strewn flour, from the corn-ships in the Orontes, over the ground to mark the direction of streets and colonnades. Alexander had laid out Alexandria in similar style, but without the elephants.[2] The city, one of sixteen Antiochs which Seleucus named after his father, was designed as a rival to this Alexandria of the Ptolemies, but never quite succeeded in being so. Its intelligentsia was inferior. Its population perhaps was too polyglot. In the fusion of East and West which was the achievement of Hellenism, Semitic life, in the long run, affected the Greeks here more than Greek life had affected the Semites.

Greek Antioch, starting its career as a capital of an empire, ended it as the capital of a small North Syrian state. In its heyday it was a city of pleasure and luxury, renowned not only for its lighting but for its plumbing. Its water supply was so plentiful that each house had several baths, while the public baths and fountains ran like rivers. It was here that Antiochus Epiphanes, the last of its notable sovereigns, liked to carouse in low company, anointed with oils and balsams.

'You are lucky, O King,' said a fellow-bather one day, 'to have so expensive a smell.'

'I will give you your fill of it,' the monarch replied, breaking the vessel of oil over his head. It ran all over the floor, so that bathers and king started falling about, laughing heartily.[3]

Antioch today is the Turkish Antakya, a bedraggled provincial town among orchards and groves of poplars, within a circle of blue-grey mountains. It affords little to the antiquarian but the clambering walls of a citadel which housed, in turn, Byzantines, Crusaders and Arabs. Its baths are murky and uninviting. Its river, the Orontes, crawls sullenly, muddily through the town, failing to give dignity to the precarious plastered houses which line its banks.

In one of these I was entertained to luncheon by an Armenian merchant, who had learnt English in a Syrian mission school. His aged mother, who presided over the meal, had survived, as a schoolgirl, the Armenian massacres in Aintab. The Turkish soldiery, she recalled,

[1] Libanius, quoted by P. H. Hitti. *History of Syria.* London: 1951.
[2] Arrian. *Anabasis.* Book III.
[3] E. S. Bouchier. *Short History of Antioch.* London: 1921.

came to abduct the girls from the school, but a fat Turkish gentleman sent them away, explaining: 'They all belong to me.' Later, as a Moslem woman was grabbing some sweets from a Christian shop, her arm was instantly withered. This was interpreted by the Turks as a sign of Allah's displeasure. Thus the Armenians were allowed to keep their possessions and to go in peace. The old lady was proud of her son, who was indeed stout and prosperous. He did good business with the Syrians, from whom he imported American cars in exchange for raisins—or more likely contraband dollars. During the Palestine war he had sold food to the Jews, and he boasted of a recent deal in which he had smuggled a Roman mosaic pavement out of the country to Australia.

'I'm a business man,' he explained.

Classical coins still abound in the bazaars of Antakya. My host advised me to beware of forgeries and introduced me to a 'reliable' dealer, a Christian. From him I bought a Roman coin, which I later discovered to be false.

* * *

Life in classical Antioch centred around the pleasure gardens of Daphne, a mile or so outside the city. 'The purest gift of the queen of nymphs',[1] it became famous far and wide as a beauty spot, hence as a place of worship and pilgrimage. Here still, among patriarchal plane-trees and mulberries, myriads of springs come gushing out of the rocks, to tumble in a bewildering headlong profusion over the smooth red earth, making an Arcadian extravaganza of grottoes and waterfalls, sparkling pools and moss-grown banks.

As a garden, Daphne was a lineal descendant of the Persian gardens, and hence, through the Jews, of the Paradise of Eden; [2] through the Romans it was perhaps an ancestor of Tivoli. As a place of worship it was licentious in character, like the oriental shrines of Astarte. Daphne herself, pursued by Apollo, had been changed into a bay-tree, and here, roofed with branches of cypress and bay, was his shrine. Bay-leaves, dipped in the stream, emerged inscribed with oracular prophecies, and a colossal statue of Apollo, playing the harp, with hair made of gold and eyes of jacinths, presided over the proceedings. 'The site and nature of the place, well-adapted to foster luxurious ease, as well as the amatory character of the legend, doubled the passions of gentry of

[1] Libanius, quoted by Hitti. *op. cit.*

[2] Hitti. *op. cit.*

corrupt mind on the least provocation. Alleging the myth as an excuse, they were still more inflamed and could not endure to see persons of respectability there.'[1] Later, in Roman times, female students at the philosophical schools wrestled with one another, scantily attired, running foot-races and delivering recitations, tragic or lyrical. The splendid cypresses, around the shrine, were preserved even by the Byzantine emperors. But when the Emperor Julian visited it in the fourth century, hoping, on the day of the feast of Apollo, to find it filled with sacrifices, 'he found not even a cake, not a grain of incense; and the god would have been without an offering had the priest himself not bought a goose'.[2]

The flavour of Daphne survives in the Roman mosaics which once decorated its villas and now decorate the Antioch Museum—another fruit of the French occupation. Late and sophisticated, with a fashionable 'Regency' air, they portray mythical scenes in which voluptuous gods and goddesses, Tritons and Nereids, nymphs and cherubs disport themselves with carefree abandon, sharing the fruits of the earth with a roistering assembly of birds and beasts and fishes.

But Daphne itself is sadly changed. Few but 'persons of respectability' go there. It is a picnic resort where, at weekends, the families of Antakya go in buses to sit in their shirt-sleeves, on upright chairs, drinking coffee and lemonade with a stolid bourgeois air. One party, I observed, had put table and chairs squarely in the water itself and sat barefoot, with rolled-up trouser-legs, dipping feet in it, without the trace of a smile. Moreover the haphazard waterfalls were being harnessed and canalized, no longer with Hadrian's elegant aqueducts, but with turbines and concrete, to provide Antioch with hydro-electric power. Thus Daphne will soon be no more.

Who cares about a lot of old waterfalls?

*   *   *

A train, luxurious after the buses of the plateau, took me away from Iskenderun, up the shores of the Gulf of Issus, then round the corner to the West into the great hot green Cilician plain. One after another we crossed the surging yellow rivers, the Pyramus and Sarus (now Ceyhan and Seyhan), and after Adana the Cydnus (now Tarsus), which carve their way down through the heart of the Taurus to spread silt over the land and enrich it. The mountains had receded well back to form an

[1] Bouchier. *op. cit.*   [2] George Finlay. *History of Greece*, London: 1876.

enveloping barrier, their crags crowned in the neighbourhood of the passes with the ruins of castles, reinforcing the defences of nature.

Stoneless, barely requiring manure, this Cilician Plain (Cilicia Campestris) is the richest corner of Asia Minor. Xenophon described it as large and beautiful, 'well-watered and full of trees of all sorts and vines', nourishing 'an abundance of sesame, millet, panic, wheat and barley',[1] Ibrahim Pasha, fresh from Egypt, added sugar to the list, and date-palms, whose trees survived, but whose fruit was uneatable. By the end of the nineteenth century cultivation had declined, and much of the plain was a marsh. Davis, however, recognized that 'this province much resembles the Delta of Egypt, and might be made in proportion equally productive'. Today, thanks to mechanization, it is almost so. Like the valley of the Nile the plain of Cilicia thrives on cotton.

Adana, set in the heart of it, is a city of cotton millionaires—a city, however, with few of the trappings of wealth. In Davis's time an Ottoman governor aspired to make Adana like the cities of Malta, where he had once lived. Unable to get funds, he deliberately set fire to it, destroying the bazaars and a quantity of slums, and rebuilding them, at a cost of some £30,000, in the style of his choice. Encouraged by the results, he was about to burn down the rest of the city, but his enemies forestalled him, and he was recalled in disgrace to Constantinople, reduced to borrowing his passage money from a Greek.

Adana could do with another conflagration. Turning its back on the Seyhan, with its fine Byzantine bridge, it is an ill-planned town, lacking in dignity, moreover innocent of Levantine splendour. Its hard-headed plutocrats, unlike the pashas of Egypt and Lebanon, do not care to flaunt their riches. The modern Turk has little taste for display. No longer does he build lavish palaces, as his forefathers did, or decorate his women with silks and jewels. He is content with an ostentatious American car, drawn up before a concrete shack of a home, and his wife drives to town in it, still in the fustian of a peasant.

I had been directed to the Cotton Palace Hotel, and here I arrived at midday on a Sunday to find the proprietor and a number of sleek friends playing cards in the hall, in their pyjamas, to the music of a gramophone. There were telephones and wash-basins in the bedrooms, but little other furniture, and I preferred the more modest prices of a nearby hotel, where the waiter kindly unclasped his pocket-knife to

[1] *Anabasis*. Book I.

spread butter on my bread at breakfast. The streets were dusty and clamorous. Since it was Sunday, only the sour-milk bars were open. I dined that night in a restaurant where a group of Americans, engaged in building a strategic aerodrome, bayed for steak and eggs-and-bacon. In a corner a contrasting group of quick refined customers mimed with delicate hands, as though absorbed in some urgent puppet drama. It concerned, as I finally overheard, the price of cotton.

Next day the shop-windows blazed with car accessories, radios, sausages, and gold. I called on a merchant, to whom I had a letter of introduction. He was a Syrian from the Sanjak, one of many still trading in this corner of Turkey, their flexibility and quickness complementing the slower and in some respects surer qualities of the Turks. After a detached analysis, shrewd and sceptical, of the present cotton 'boom', he took me to luncheon at a club where the plutocrats gathered. Here I met the head of the local farmers' union—a union of landowners. The large landowner has disappeared from the greater part of Turkey, his lands divided among the peasants by Atatürk's agrarian Socialist policy. Here around Adana he still survives, his estates combined for all practical purposes with those of his brothers and uncles and moreover producing a higher yield than elsewhere. Side by side with him, however, the small peasant proprietor still cultivates his land—and indeed I was assured by my host that the quality of his cotton, well-tended and picked, is superior to that of the big landowners.

I was not sorry to leave Adana. Here is Turkey at its most prosperous—but not always at its best. Before doing so I called on the aged mother of a friend, a noted politician. One of the Young Turks of his day, a product of Atatürk's revolution nourished on the more truly Turkish soil of the Taurus, he had developed into a man of wide European culture, with an international sense spreading far beyond its peaks and valleys. A true democrat, he accepted with a philosophic shrug the fact that he was now a leader of the Opposition, the People's Party of Atatürk, and likely to remain so for some time to come. For the Democrat Party had lately increased its majority at the elections, and now dominated the country against a Parliamentary Opposition unhealthily small. Ironically, the two-party system in Turkey seemed in effect to be continuing one-party rule—by the free choice of the people itself. It has since been modified, perhaps more healthily, by a split among the Democrats and the emergence of other parties.

My friend had transported his mother from the land of his fathers to a fine modern house, all concrete and steel, in the city, where he could visit her more easily. Here she sat, wearing flat-heeled peasant shoes and a kerchief around her head, gazing out over the streamlined Seyhan barrage, and swaying gently to and fro as she talked in a deep resonant voice of her son. With her ample loins and hieratic profile she seemed the incarnation of the mother-goddess, a symbol of the eternal earth-woman, looking on a strange new world in a spirit of resigned acceptance, tinged with maternal pride, but still with her roots deep down in the Anatolian soil.

* * *

The plain of Adana is one of those points on the coast of Asia Minor, where, as Sykes puts it, 'the littoral chain breaks inland, thus enlarging coast conditions',[1] hence where the peoples of the sea have found a permanent foothold inland. Originally it was more Phoenician than Greek—an outpost of Syria rather than of Europe. The name of Cilicia derives, as Herodotus records, from Cilix, the son of Agenor, a Phoenician King.[2] It seems that he settled here, about the middle of the sixteenth century B.C., preferring the rich fruits of the plain to a continued and tedious search for his sister Europa, who had been carried off by pirates. The name of Tarsus, for centuries its principal city, is clearly Semitic, derived from the Phoenician name Tarshish. The prophet Isaiah describes Tyre as a 'daughter of Tarshish',[3] thus suggesting that it was a colony of Cilicia.

But the Greeks were here too, at an early stage in Cilician history—or so, at a later stage, they were at some pains to claim. Traditionally their colonies of Mopsuestia and Mallus dated back to the Trojan War, founded by Mopsus and Amphilochus, two mythical prophets and heroes of Troy, who killed one another in a dispute over their Cilician sovereignty and were buried one out of sight of the other, lest the feud should continue.[4] Alexander gave credence to the legend by sacrificing to the shades of Amphilochus at Mallus, and remitting its tribute in view of its connection, which he shared, with the Argives.[5] An eighth-century inscription at Karatepe does indeed record the existence of a King 'of the house of Mopsus', ruling over the plain of

[1] Sir Mark Sykes. *The Caliph's Lost Heritage*. London: 1915.

[2] *History*. Book VII.

[3] Isaiah xxiii. 10.

[4] Strabo. *Geography*. Book XIV.

[5] *Arrian Anabasis*. Book II.

Adana, and from the seventh century onwards Greek colonial activity in Cilicia is a matter of historical fact.[1] Tarsus became a colony of the Ionians, though, as late as the second century A.D., it was described still as 'more like a Phoenician than a Hellenic city'.[2] Walled in by the Taurus, the great plain of Cilicia has in any event nourished, throughout long periods of its history, civilizations different from those of the lands above it, whether Hittite or Phrygian, Persian or Turkish.

During the Christian period, easy of access from Syria across the Amanus, it was occupied on and off by the infidel Arabs—those raiding dynasties, with an advanced headquarters at Tarsus, which tried year after year to conquer the plateau, but were defeated by the more formidable Taurus. Later the mountains served as a barrier between Christianity and Islam in the inverse sense. Cilicia was for three hundred years the Christian Kingdom of Lesser Armenia, the final refuge of a people driven from their homes on the plateau, and at the same time a thoroughfare for the Crusaders. It stood out against the Turks in the North, thanks to the chain of fortresses which I had seen from the plain and of which I was to see more as I travelled westwards; and indeed it was conquered eventually not by the Turks but by the Mamelukes from the South. The Turks held the plateau for centuries, before mastering Cilicia, and in fact, as Ramsay has pointed out, occupied Belgrade before they occupied Tarsus.[3] In his day there was still a strong distinction between the racial character of the plateau and that of the plain. In Cilicia, he remarked, 'you detect at once the impression of the Arab and the Ansarieh, you hear yourself no longer addressed as Tchelebi, which was practically universal as a title of respect before you crossed Taurus: the people now style you Hawaja, as in Syria and Egypt'.

Today, with the Turkification, at least on the surface, of the remaining Arabs, following the virtual disappearance of the Greeks, the distinction is less marked. But it exists nevertheless in the more polyglot nature of the coastal Turks, and in the survival in the towns of an influential Syrian element, preserving its racial identity.

* * *

[1] Michael Gough, appendix to Mary Gough. *The Plain and the Rough Places.* London: 1954.

[2] Dion Chrysostom, quoted by *Encyclopaedia Britannica.*

[3] Sir William Ramsay in *Royal Geographical Society Journal.* London: September 1902.

I avoided Tarsus, where little survives of the past, content with a glimpse of its muddy river, the Cydnus, where Cleopatra sat in her barge on the way up to meet Antony. It was a journey which won her rich tracts of Cilician pasture-lands, cedar-forests and iron mines, together with a serviceable harbour. As the Taurus drew nearer to the plain, my train turned southwards, reaching the port of Mersin. In Davis's time this was 'a few wretched huts', built on piles to escape the malaria which raged here. But it began to recover, shipping wheat during the Crimean War, and since World War II has prospered further, reaping the fruits of American aid to Turkey. Today it consists of a few streets of smug prosperous concrete villas, decked with bougainvillea and looking out on to a municipal sea-front, where palms strive valiantly to survive the salt sea-spray. Its happy fate, as planned, is to be the leading port on the south coast of Turkey—but only if the land can be kept at bay. Swollen by bountiful mud from the Taurus, it encroaches on the sea in a relentless methodical advance; the harbour is deep with silt, and the ships must lie out in the roadstead.

Meanwhile the people of Mersin profit by its bounty—a mixed commercial population, predominantly Turkish, but including Syrians, Lebanese, Armenians, some Frenchmen and Italians—and even a few surviving Greeks. Around the city drainage and irrigation have transformed fever swamps and undisciplined scrub into ordered groves of citrus. A chemist, glad to escape from his shop in the heat of the day, took me out to a plot of land refreshed by a perceptible sea-breeze, which had made him a capitalist. His shop brought him an income of £100 a month; his land brought him another £250, all he could possibly need, with a nice sum left over to invest in Mersin house property. His trees were aglow with lemons and oranges, as with great round lamps weighing down their branches, and the ground was gold with windfalls. He knew and loved each tree, showing off their variety, tending them, evening after evening, from a house which he had built among them, rejoicing in his new-found peasant role. As a chemist, he knew that grapefruit was rich in Vitamin B, and gave me a deep cool draught of its juice. Its roots, when boiled, he declared, cure kidney-trouble.

Across the road was a rich merchant's estate, with groves which marched over well-tended acres, in regular formation, towards the foot of the Taurus. But a sudden cruel breeze, sweeping down from the snows, had struck rank after rank of them dead. The owners, as they drove me around it next day in a cream-coloured Cadillac with green silken upholstery, were not greatly disturbed. The estate, it seemed, was a mere plaything, the social symbol of a wealth which was solidly founded on trade.

This trade until a generation ago was almost entirely in the hands of the Syrians and Greeks—Greeks who in the eyes of the nineteenth-century traveller did not count as Europeans, since Davis, in writing of them, adds that the unhealthy climate and lax commercial morality of Mersin made it impossible for Europeans to thrive there. The Turks at this time seem to have been largely a floating population of camel-drivers. Now commercially they have come into their own, out-numbering the foreigners.

I met only a single Greek in Mersin: a merchant who, in the exodus of 1922, had left this coast to settle in Cyprus, and had now come over to buy vetch, beans and sesame. Like so many of his race he was a man of gusto, who saw life as a game. He found uproarious drama in the tedious incidents of commercial dealing, and recounted, at the expense of the Turks, a rich comic odyssey of everyday experiences. Exposed to his ruthless talent for pantomime, they became, with their haphazard business methods and bureaucratic ways, sad figures of fun. After a thousand years of so wounding an attitude, it was perhaps understandable that they finally drove the Greeks into the sea.

CHAPTER 2

CILICIA (2)

The Pirate Coast—Pompeiopolis—A Roman Built-up Area—An Armenian Castle—Cilician Sports—The Corycian Caves—The End of an Emperor—Anamur—Up into the Taurus—Ermenek—A Friend of the British

CILICIA TRACHEA (the Rough Land), where the wall of the Taurus closes in once and for all on the coast, is with its rocky capes and sheltered creeks a historic home of piracy. As dynasties have decayed so have the pirates, indigenous to the country, flourished. Thus in the declining days of the Hellenistic era there had grown up here, and in the neighbouring Pamphylia, in alliance with the cities of Crete, a pirate confederation so powerful that it virtually controlled the Eastern Mediterranean. The pirates captured hundreds of cities, built fortified harbours and signal stations, pillaged shrines and carried off wealthy Roman citizens for ransom. They grew rich through their exportation of slaves to the Romans themselves, mainly to the island of Delos which, according to Strabo, was 'a large and rich mart, capable of receiving and transporting, when sold, the same day, ten thousand slaves'.[1] Hence, he adds, arose the proverbial saying: 'Merchant, come into port, discharge your freight—everything is sold.' The Romans, to crush the power of the pirates, had finally to launch a major campaign under Pompey, who subdued them, capturing more than eight hundred ships and twenty thousand prisoners.[2] With some vision, Pompey realized that their lawlessness was due largely to poor social and economic conditions. Thus he re-settled them in various under-populated cities. One of these was Adana; another was Soli.

This easterly outpost of the Greeks was a colony of Rhodes and

[1] *Geography*. Book XIV.
[2] T. R. S. Broughton. *Roman Asia Minor*. Baltimore: 1938.

perhaps of the Argives. 'A considerable city',[1] it had enjoyed the status of an independent Kingdom under the Assyrians and again under the Persians, and was rich enough to pay Alexander a substantial fine for its collaboration with the enemy. Through the ages the speech of its inhabitants had grown so corrupt as to earn the name of solecism—a doubtful honour claimed also by the colony of Soli, in Cyprus. Now Soli, thanks presumably to the ravages of the pirates, was in decay. Pompey rebuilt it and named it Pompeiopolis.

The Vice-Consul in Mersin motored me out to inspect its ruins: the relics of an avenue of slender Corinthian columns, stretching up from the sea towards a Turkish village in the foothills of the Taurus; substantial fragments of classical buildings, lying scattered over the stony ploughland. The Romans brought water in an aqueduct from the hills down to the harbour, where ships took it on board. Their quays and moles, built of a rough conglomerate like concrete, survive for the most part indestructible, their massive blocks, now overgrown with seaweed, joined together with clamps of iron. Around us the peasants were building houses from the profits of their cotton. They built by cautious stages, a storey a year: a makeshift outside ladder one year, an inside staircase the next. Bulgarian Moslem families, from behind the Iron Curtain, were being settled on land, still undeveloped, nearby. Pushed across the frontier in large numbers, in order to embarrass the Turkish government, they were proving on the contrary an asset to this underpopulated country. Thus no more were now being released. The new policy was to keep them in Bulgaria and indoctrinate them with Communism.

Next day I continued my journey, westwards by bus along the rock-bound sea-coast. Soon the land reverted to scrub and brushwood, and few inhabitants were to be seen. But some of it seemed worthy of cultivation, and sure enough we came presently into the outskirts of what was evidently once a thriving city. For mile after mile it lined the roadside, in effect a Roman built-up area of vast extent. Utterly deserted, overgrown with lentiscus, scattered with carobs and wild olives which must once have been cultivated, were the ruins of imposing public buildings. A weathered rock would suddenly assume the features of a Roman pediment, a massive boulder would become the drum of an Ionic column. But the dwellings of the dead, ostentatious tombs and vaults and sarcophagi, outnumbered those of the living.

[1] Strabo. *op. cit.*

This is the city to which Strabo[1] refers as Elaeussa. Built on an island which has since silted up into a peninsula, it was 'the holy, the inviolable, the self-governing mistress of ships,' [2] the centre of a Roman Kingdom conferred by Antony on Archelaus and re-named Sebaste.

Behind it, an imposing product of Roman engineering, a long aqueduct is slung like a chain from slope to slope, to bring water from the Taurus. Farther west, in the more thickly populated area of Üzümburç, forty miles of a similar Roman aqueduct have been cleaned and repaired by the Turks to supply a number of villages, which were formerly as much as thirty-five miles from their water. The cost was but a fraction of the half-million pounds which modern engineering would have demanded. The original cost to the Romans was the labour of some fifteen hundred prisoners.

From these relics of Rome we came suddenly round a corner, to find ourselves in the Middle Ages. Here, commanding the flawless curve of a bay, stood the castle of Corycus, its walls and towers white and gold against water so shallow that its ripples were reflected, like gold-mesh netting, on the sand. Corycus, once doubtless Byzantine, was a castle of the Armenians. It is a redoubtable fortress, with a moat, and double walls, and a massive sea-gate opening direct on to the Mediterranean. The people of this coast looked seaward rather than landward, and it is a narrower gate which leads out to the rocky mountainside behind. Within the castle precincts black goats grazed amid a tangle of wild olives. Here the ruins of two churches survive, of which one is Gothic, Crusader in style, and there are Armenian inscriptions to be seen.

When the last King of Armenia, Leo VI of the Lusignan family, was on the run before the Mamelukes, Corycus, defended by Genoese merchant troops, was one of the fortresses which held out. Leo finally escaped into exile, to Cyprus, to Italy, to Castile, to France, to England. After trying in vain to persuade the Kings of France and England (Richard II) to launch a new Crusade for the recovery of his Kingdom, he settled down comfortably in Paris, on handsome pensions from both of them. He died in 1393, leaving no successor, and was borne to a black marble tomb in the church of the Celestines, 'clothed in royal robes of white . . . with an open crown upon his head and a golden sceptre in his hand'.[3]

[1] *Geography*. Book V

[2] From a Roman coin. Quoted by Gough. *op. cit.*

[3] Robert Curzon. *Armenia*. London: 1854.

In this wild rocky country the inhabitants of Mersin pursue game for the market, mainly francolin and red-legged partridge, much as the Crusaders must have done for the pot. Their methods are ingenious. Salted grain is spread by the water, where the birds come to drink. They eat it, and the grain swells inside them until they can hardly move. Thus they are easily captured. Alternatively a caged female is placed as a decoy; the males come to admire her, and are shot where they sit. Barker described a similar method a century ago. Then a cock was placed in the cage, and as it crowed other male birds came to fight it. 'It is remarkable', he writes, 'that the cock will eat the brains of its fallen enemy, which are generally given to it; and it is curious to see it crow and quite glut itself as if triumphing in its repast.' [1] Another method was to exhaust the birds by galloping them down on horseback, then catching them with the hand. Quails are caught here when they crash in flight into white-painted boards, well lit from the foot; or the hunter imitates an eagle, with broad wings of black cloth, throwing a shadow on the ground from which they scuttle in fear into a net.

On an island off Corycus, like a crown of stone on the sea, stands a second mediaeval castle, romantic in its aspect, of which the Turks tell a story: [2] 'The King of Korykos . . . had an only daughter of peerless beauty of whom it was prophesied at her birth that she would die of the bite of a snake. To avert this catastrophe the King built a castle upon the island and there he kept his daughter virtually a prisoner. But Fate was not to be baulked and a snake accidentally introduced in a basket of vegetables proved the prophecy true.'

Some relation to the asp of Cleopatra?

* * *

By the effigy of a headless Roman soldier, carved on a tomb by the roadside, I waited for the bus to take me westwards. Here the white cliffs of Cilicia surge up, as though in motion, from the brink of the sea: light, living masses of cavernous limestone, organic with the shells and bones of the marine creatures which helped to form them. Soft and pliable, they allow the elements to sculpt them, creating curious quirks and freaks of nature. Driving around a headland into a small still cove we were confronted with a portent. A herd of cattle was drinking

[1] W. B. Barker, *Cilicia and its Governors*. London: 1853.

[2] John Thomson. *Castles in Cilicia. The Geographical Magazine*. London: April 1951.

placidly out of the sea itself. This was no hallucination, but a natural phenomenon. Fresh water had seeped down through the porous rock, to gush upwards once more from beneath the sea-bed, flooding the sea with sweet cool springs.

Above this spot, at Narli Kuyu, two caverns have scooped themselves out of the land. Tradition has named them Heaven and Hell, the respective homes of Zeus and the giant Typhon, and doubtless of earlier deities. Typhon was the legendary 'Cilician hundred-headed monster and the King of the giants',[1] who 'withstood all the gods, hissing out terror with horrid jaws, while his eyes lighted a hideous glare',[2] and who sought to challenge their sovereignty. Inevitably Zeus, with his 'unsleeping bolt', got the better of him, reducing him to ashes, and transferring him to the belly of Mount Etna, whence 'a monster in bondage', he still breathes flame.[3]

The cave of the giant opened abruptly at my feet, more crater than cave, perhaps a quarter of a mile round, wide open and so deep that the stone which I flung into it took four seconds to reach the bottom. Encircled by a precipice, streaked with iron, the chasm is inaccessible to the traveller. Only birds, like bats with crimson-hued cloaks, fly silently amid its profusion of ferns and scrub, making a cry like the chipping of stone. In the time of Strabo the place was noted for its saffron, derived from the autumn crocus.

The cave of the God is appropriately nobler than that of the monster. Rugged in structure, majestic in span, it slopes gradually down towards the centre of the earth, the pink glare of the sunlight slowly receding, a blue light beckoning from the depths. With its bold wide soaring nave of limestone it is a welcoming cavern, its steps polished gold, its rock face soaked and speckled and slashed with nature's mixture of blues and pinks and yellows. Silence fills it, broken only by the echoing twitter of a bird outside. But as the vault grows narrower and the darkness descends, there comes from the deep, still-distant bowels of the rock a low continuous roar. Here is the source of Strabo's underground river 'of pure and transparent water'. At the brink of the cave, as though to propitiate the unknown spirits which lurk in the depths of the earth, the Christians have built a rough chapel, where pagan shrines may have stood, and where a Byzantine inscription contrasts with earlier inscriptions, to Corycian Zeus and Hermes.

[1] Strabo. *Geography*. Book XIV.

[2] Aeschylus. *Prometheus Bound.*

[3] Pindar, *Pythian Odes*. I.

At Silifke, the ancient Seleucia, we crossed without mishap the swirling milk-yellow rapids of the Calycadnus, which drowned the Emperor Frederick Barbarossa. Crossing the Taurus from Karaman, on the Third Crusade, he rode ahead of the army, with his bodyguard. What happened when he reached the river is largely conjecture. Plunging in for a bathe, he may well have succumbed to the shock of the ice-cold water. The waters of the Cydnus, after all, had almost killed in this fashion a younger monarch, Alexander the Great, as he washed off the dust of his passage through the Cilician Gates. In any event the army arrived to find the corpse of their Emperor stretched on the bank. The accident was fateful to the Crusade, and was interpreted by Saladin as a sign from Heaven. The body of the Emperor was carried by his troops through the damp heat of the Cilician Plain, preserved ineffectively in vinegar. Starting to decay, it was hastily buried in the cathedral at Antioch, certain bones being removed to travel on with the army, towards the Holy Land.[1]

The icy waters of Cilicia were fatal in a different sense to the son of Harun al Rashid, al Mamun. Resting by a stream, after the exertion of capturing fifteen towns, he expressed a longing for some dates from his native land, to complete his felicity. At that moment, by a remarkable coincidence, a caravan of mules passed by, carrying dates fresh from Baghdad. Two baskets of these were placed before him. He ate them up, drinking copiously from the waters of the stream. Presently he was seized with a fever, and died.[2]

The rock which looks down on the Calycadnus, now the Göksu, is girded by the ruins of a feudal castle, its walls bowing with dignity towards the Mediterranean. From here I was driven westwards in a Land-Rover by a sturdy inspector from the Ministry of Agriculture, who spoke little but now and then laughed. His loudest laugh followed the discovery that my bag, containing all my clothes, had jolted itself out of the car at some bend in the road, and might well have vanished over a precipice. Recovering his composure, he assured me that in so efficient and law-abiding a country the bag would be discovered and returned to me within the next few days or weeks. The gendarmerie might require a little time to search the mountainside. But I need not fear. At that moment, to my relief, another car caught up with us, containing the bag, which had been found on the road.

[1] Steven Runciman. *History of the Crusades*, Vol. III. London: 1954.

[2] Barker. *op. cit.*

It was a wild tumultuous landscape which now crowded around us, making the road twist eternally as it forced its passage between the Taurus range and the sea: a cyclopean rock-garden, joyous with colour, elbowing its way out to sea and thrusting strong rough arms around bays of a shimmering stillness. Here and there it made way for a broad red valley, its spacious hillsides blue with olive trees, purple with fruit trees, green with holly and cistus. But their terraces were crumbling. It was an empty landscape.

'*Adam yok*,' said my escort: no Adams, no men: a cry familiar enough in this land generous by nature, barren only under protest, through man's desertion.

Until Atatürk's time this was a coast of Greek traders, where two or three small ports flourished, each on its own, like the city states of the past. Now the ports are dead places, though the Turks have a plan to revive Tasuçu, as an outlet for Silifke and the cities of the plateau, up the valley of the Göksu. We lunched at Gilindire, once Celenderis, then a colony of Phoenician Greeks, now a somnolent village with a few ruins and a fistful of rocks protecting its harbour. Beyond it the landscape, lonelier than ever, reverted to virgin pine-forest, light and feminine in its freshness and in its fine-spun needle design. Rampaging downwards in an unbridled turmoil of boulders and scree and scrub, the mountains flung out a progression of bluff gold crags, which advanced and withdrew from the silent sea as in some buoyant rhythmic ballet. Receding, they soared into a pinnacle, which man had defended with double walls and bastions, then pranced off with a flourish, giving way to the plain of Anamur, where bananas grew in sub-tropical profusion.

Here my companion dropped me at the Banana Palas Otel, and, in teeming rain, hurried onwards over hazardous uncompleted roads to Alanya. Typical of the young Turkish technicians of today, he was a man dedicated to his work, for ever travelling on tours of inspection over a wide and arduous country. Anamur is the southernmost point of Asia Minor. Perhaps the remotest village on this lonely coast, it is still badly served by roads and hence by buses. I was anxious to travel up from the coast into the Taurus, to Ermenek, and for this would need the help of official transport. I therefore called next day on the *Kaymakam* in the bleak white government office which dwarfed the village. A solemn youth with a sallow, almost Indian complexion and long black eyelashes, he was polite enough to detain me for an hour and a quarter, begging me to remain while he transacted his daily business. First he opened the letters which lay piled on his desk, and sent them away to be read—a curious reversal of western office practice. Then, trying to look older than his years, he extended a gentle patronage towards a series of mature visitors, pressing a frequent bell for cups of coffee, which were brought by a tie-less greybeard. Through the ever-open door they wandered in unannounced: a local member of Parliament, stout and urban in aspect; his predecessor, thin, drawn, old and military; persons poor and deferential, presenting papers to be signed; deputations, telling confused contradictory stories.

The *Kaymakam* dealt with all concurrently, turning first to one suppliant, then to another, then to me, then to the M.P., then back to the first, with impartial courtesy. Those with no apparent business to do stayed longest, preparing the way perhaps for future favours, or trying to find out something without appearing to do so. The implied assumption was that all, including myself, had plenty of time to spare. Finally, interrupting his hearing of a petition, the *Kaymakam* turned to me with the news for which I had patiently hoped. Arrangements would be made for me to go to Ermenek. He would take me himself. He did not say when. I thanked him sincerely, and left in the charge of a young official, an agriculturist with a Hittite nose, a flat back to his head and a front tooth missing, who seemed happily unaware of these defects. In his costume he showed a whimsical taste for variety—double-breasted pin-stripe jacket, no tie, check plus-fours to the ankle, rubber shoes, green socks, and a crimson pullover. It presented a striking contrast with the photograph of Atatürk on the wall, in impeccable evening dress. He drove me in a jeep to the ruins of Anemorium, lying at the foot of the Cape which juts out into the sea towards Cyprus. Above us a battle was being waged in the sky. A large owl, like a night bomber too slow for the daylight, was being attacked by two falcons, wheeling around it like Spitfires, pecking viciously at its head. But it lumbered onwards, apparently unperturbed, until they abandoned the chase.

Anemorium, in Roman and Byzantine times, must have been a city of imposing size. Today little remains of the city of the living, whose stones and columns may, as Beaufort [1] suggests, have been carried off to Cyprus. But a vast city of the dead survives, dead who must in life have been rich and respected, since their tombs are like mansions, street after street of them, with well-built domes and vaults and pavements.

[1] Francis Beaufort. *Karamania*. London: 1818.

The ridge which dominates the city is belted with the walls of a Byzantine citadel, and with two Roman aqueducts, their masonry still to a great extent intact. They brought water from the mountains, fifteen miles off, to fill the fountains and baths of the city, and could easily be repaired by the Turks to bring it again, and so to irrigate the fields which now cover the site of it. Today their crops, of sesame and beans and wheat, depend on the rain, and it was with hope in his eyes that my quaintly-dressed guide watched the gathering darkening clouds. They bore down on the plain, creating a tropical sultriness; and indeed, within the shelter of its encircling mountains, Anamur is a pocket of perennial warmth. Among the ruins anemones, yellow and mauve, were breaking into flower in a rash November spring.

The inhabitants assured me that Anamur knew no winter, and that if I remained here I could bathe happily from Easter until Christmas. The town, in its shabby lethargy, offered me little inducement to do so. My agriculturist gave me lunch in its only eating-house, preceded by glasses of a sweet tangerine liqueur. No knives were provided, and we tore at our chicken with spoon and fork, washing it down with lukewarm beer and counteracting its taste with bananas. The proprietor was in features a Mongol, the waiter a dumb Mediterranean ox, the scullion a negroid boy. After sitting for an hour or so in silence, in front of emptying bottles of beer, we drove to the castle of Anamur, on the eastern side of the bay. Alone on the sand, with a soft sea lapping at its bold serrated ramparts, it has a romantic dignity unmatched by other fortresses on this turbulent pirate coast. A castle within a castle, colossal in scale, its long battlements, still unbroken, face sea and land with a calm, robust assurance. Three great gateways pierce the walls which, within and without, are ringed in symmetry with towers and bastions, now polygonal, now circular, now square. In the outer courtyard is a domed brick mosque, and nearby the remains of an aqueduct from the mountains. The Seljuk defenders of the castle evolved a system of signalling by torchlight, over the peaks of the Taurus to the plateau beyond, by which the garrison of Konya—a hundred miles off as the crow flies—could be swiftly warned of an attack. On a neighbouring elbow of rock stands a fort, the first stage in the relay, while the brow of a more distant peak is crowned with a larger fortress, like a chaplet of stone.

Rearing skywards from among a cortège of satellites, formed in its image, the range of the Taurus processed inland as though with a beckoning gesture. Next day, in a truck, with the Hittite-nosed agriculturist and three of his colleagues, but without the *Kaymakam*, we climbed up over its smooth elephantine flanks towards a ridge like a granite breastplate, ribbed with gold. Soon the sea, far beneath us, was no more than a disc of dappled silver. The rock-hewn limestone slopes, instinct with movement, deployed around us, rank upon rank, in an ever-changing perspective of light and colour and form. An ice-green river, cleaving its way down between their haunches, washed the rocks with red earth, giving life to paps of a gentler green fertility. The shoulders of the ridge were cloaked with pine-forest and, higher still, with cedars, the dry bark flaking from their corrugated trunks. But beyond it, where the snows would soon descend, we came abruptly into a derelict world. Here, skidding away towards a bleak horizon, was an undulating wilderness of splintered stone, its sparse trees stunted and warped by the ruthless axe, or dead already, gaunt, grotesque and naked. Bereft of dignity and support, their roots exposed above layers of tired white earth, they had the air of slipping helplessly downhill.

A river-bed, tumbling with smooth white stones, awaited the first winter torrent. And here, in a cold breeze, forgetting the tropics of yesterday, we lunched by a trough of ice-cold water. Nearby was a *yayla*, where the shepherds in summer grazed their herds, and remorselessly ploughed the thin earth which survived. Its deserted village glared at us coldly, and the door of a house, left unlocked, banged with nagging repetition, as it would continue to do throughout the lonely monotonous winter. The inhabitants had migrated to the plains and valleys, stripping the trees of their branches to keep them warm in the winter, as they went. Here was a rich mountain reduced to penury, not by war's devastation but by man's improvident neglect.

At the most desolate spot we dropped one of our party, a young man in breeches, with umbrella and brief-case, who set off alone into the void to an unseen village—a modern St. Paul of the welfare state. But soon the valley of the Göksu opened beneath us, deep and broad and shadowed with purple. Perched on the edge of it, facing the wind from the North, was a flat-roofed village in a landscape licked by the last flames of autumn—trees flaring and guttering, yellow and gold, against a sunlit rose-pink opposite slope. The river forms the boundary with another province, that of Konya, and my companions, as though facing an unknown foreign land, seemed strangely reluctant to cross it.

The local schoolmaster entertained us to coffee, in his room without a table, with only a mattress on the floor and papers piled on the window-sill, but with walls tastefully stencilled with bouquets of flowers. In these bleak surroundings, where all felt at home, they urged that we spend the night, instead of venturing into the alien land of Ermenek. With some impatience I refused. So we wound our way down to the pallid river, across a bridge where it narrowed to force a passage through towering cliffs, and up the kinder southern slope, where the rocks flushed pink in the sunset.

Ermenek is one of the highest villages in the Taurus. Once Germanicopolis, it was a settlement established, with some enterprise, among the barbarous Cilicians, by Antiochus IV Epiphanes, on behalf of his masters, the Romans. Shut firmly off from the North and its winds by a concave wall of rock, the village curves high around the neck of it, an architectural collar of earthy sand-gold stone and rough bleached timber, well adorned with vines and fruit trees. Davis disliked the place, complaining that there was 'little or nothing to do or see, and the people are rude and over-reaching. Even the baker, who promised faithfully to give us some pure wheaten bread, and was paid accordingly, gave us the same abominable stuff with which the Smyrniote Greeks have inundated the whole province.'

I had no such unfortunate experience. Contrary to the parochial fears of my friends, we were given a cordial welcome by the Mayor of Ermenek, who put his house at our disposal for the night. Mattresses and quilts were spread for us on the carpeted floor of the living-room, beneath a low cushioned window-seat which overlooked the view. The Mayor's ladies had embroidered the pillows with pansies, and the cushions with bright designs in apricot, crimson and green. There were ewers and basins of silvered copper, and the walls, surmounted by a scroll-patterned cornice of sweet-smelling wood, were hung with family photographs—a holy man, a schoolboy, a soldier—each in a garland of artificial flowers. The room was aromatic with the scent of the timber and of drying fruits and corn-cobs. We slept well, lulled by the sounds of rushing streams outside.

In the morning the Mayor's cousin, a plump round-headed boy in a thick cloth cap, brought a breakfast of thin peasant bread, like felt, with rich honey and a sheep's-milk cheese. Beneath us the landscape, glowing through curtains of gold and crimson leaves, swept down to the valley, now filled with a soft mist like some encroaching arm of the sea. Wandering through the single cobbled street in the light cool morning air, I was accosted in English by a lanky individual wearing spectacles and a shabby black overcoat. His forehead receded sharply, his voice was thin and deferential, and he had the musty air of a Dickensian clerk who has known better days. He had, he said, risen from his sick-bed to greet me, being an admirer of the British, who had taken him prisoner in the First World War.

'War is bad,' I suggested.

'No,' he said. 'War is good.' He had spent it with the English in Egypt, Palestine, Malta, and finally in England itself. But alas! until today he had seen no Englishman for twenty-eight years. Then one had come to Ermenek.

'He was a *Konsolos* from Mersin. You are a *Konsolos*?'

'No. I am writing a book.'

'Then, please, you will put me in your book.'

I would make no promises. He took me to his garden, an unkempt tangle of fruit trees, and gave me a withered apple.

'Now,' he said, dropping his voice with appropriate respect, 'we will go to see the Director of the Municipality, the Supreme Judge, the Adjutant to the Governor.' He bowed instinctively at each high-sounding title.

Mercifully a lorry was waiting, to take me northwards. Behind the wall which sheltered Ermenek we were back in an ashen desolation. Soon the land was stripped once more to its bones, but for a single decayed limb at which a herd of black goats gnawed like a relentless swarm of maggots. By the roadside a peasant had rashly left a treasured hoard of winter firewood. Our driver stopped, whisked it on board, and drove on.

CHAPTER 3

PISIDIA AND PAMPHYLIA

The Lake of Eğridir—A Hurried Excursion—Antalya and its Gardens—Mount Climax—Classical Cities of the Coast—A Roman Skyscraper—Termessus and its Theatre

IT WAS SUMMER when I next travelled down from the plateau to the coastal lands beneath the Taurus. For two long days I drove over its weary surface in a pillar of dust, first to Kutahya, with its castle and its factory where the 'Rhodian' pottery is made, but now in sadly degenerate colours, patterns and shapes; then to Afyon Karahissar, with its giddy sugar-loaf fortress of iron-stone and its shops festooned with sausages. From here, through Pisidia, the landscape falls towards the sea in a procession of slow broad steps, flooded with light. No trace of a river assists its descent, for here the waters from the Taurus bury themselves underground, emerging only for a spell, in a series of landlocked lakes, then once more vanishing from sight.

The tiers of wheat-land, with their park-like trees, were still green. The lake of Burdur shone, mile after mile, like a long blue inland gulf—a lake filled with arsenic, hence bereft of fish. I made a detour to the lake of Eğridir, a fathomless fresh-water sea, nourishing fish in abundance, which the Turks export to Syria. Sea-green in colour, deepening to jade as the sun mounts into the sky, and flecked by waves as by a flaw in the jade, it lies alone within an enclave of coral-pink mountains, their rains and snows seeping into it the whole year through. Towards the South it finds an outlet among reeds and trees wreathed with a riot of vines, their leaf-green freshness clashing with the water like the flare of new silk against the sheen of old metal. On a promontory, facing an island like an Asiatic *Toten Insel*, I explored the battered walls of a small Seljuk city, containing a handsome mosque and *medresse* and the ruins of a distinguished house. Once inhabited by some Ottoman pasha, it is now the home of hens and goats. The inherent elegance of Turkish nineteenth-century taste survives its decay, in the faded blues and pinks of painted panels, in the carving of a balcony, the curve of an alcove, the intimate grace of a courtyard, with rooms giving on to the lake.

Beyond Burdur a stream welled up to the surface, giving nourishment to orchards, strangely profuse, between eroded bare-backed hills. Soon it vanished, and the landscape reverted to stone, until over a crest the first Mediterranean breeze swept up to it from the South, restoring moisture and colour and life. As the road wound downwards into Pamphylia, the warm air was sweetened by cistus and pine. Down in the plain the water gushed once more to the surface in a great spring known to the Greeks as Katarrhactes. Yet again it disappeared, condemning the plain behind Antalya to the aridity of an African prairie. But at last, by the port, it emerged once and for all in a multitude of cataracts, plunging into the sea with a reckless sparkling exuberance.

The first time I made this journey I was the guest of old and hospitable friends, a family of Ottoman Turkish origin who lived, still in the grand manner, in an *art nouveau* palace on the Bosporus. We travelled in style, but always in a hurry, in two Cadillacs, with a doctor and a butler, who was for ever donning a white coat to serve lavish picnic meals, with cigars to follow. In Antalya my host and his son, not given to sight-seeing, sat all day long in a coffee-shop, while my hostess and the doctor and I visited the Roman and Greek cities of the coast, planning to visit next day the mountain city of Termessus.

But my host, at the end of his day in the coffee-shop, remembered the need to reach a reliable telephone, in case some urgent message awaited him in Istanbul. So at five o'clock next morning we set off once more for the plateau, crossing it hour after hour in our pillar of dust, stopping only late in the afternoon for a picnic lunch, until finally, towards midnight, we smelt the Sea of Marmara. When I confessed periodically to hunger I was reminded that I had, after all, endured the rigours of war, and my retort that even armies marched on their stomachs provoked merely incredulous laughter. Our journey, in a single day, across all Anatolia from the Mediterranean to the Sea of Marmara, was a remarkable testimonial not only to Ottoman endurance but to modern Turkish roads: roads which now make possible a regular service of light lorries from Antalya to the Bosporus, from one climate to another, providing Istanbul with early fruit and vegetables, and lorry-owners with a hundred per cent profit. But this consoled me little for my all too brief glimpse of Antalya and its surrounding classical cities. Now, alone for a few days and therefore not in a hurry, I could at last explore them at leisure.

* * *

Antalya was in Ottoman times Adalia—often a seat of some unruly autonomous pasha, defying the central government. When Beaufort approached it in 1811 he found himself involved in an abortive revolt against one of these pashas by his brother, a nominee of the Porte; and though 'cold and calculating prudence' forbade him to involve His Majesty's flag, humanity finally induced him to take a party of fugitives on board his frigate. In the following year he went into Adalia, where his appearance—such was British prestige—caused some disquiet. The Turkish officer who came on board 'peeped into the storerooms and cabins with amusing anxiety, as if apprehensive, at every door, that a new pasha would step out'. In return for a present of bullocks, goats, fowls and vegetables from the Bey, who had succeeded his father, Beaufort sent ashore 'a small cask of gunpowder, some dozens of ale and porter, and a few trifling articles of English manufacture: the cask and the basket were ornamented with green, the sacred colour of the Turks; and were carried on poles, by ten of the most athletic and handsome men of our crew . . . calculated . . . to excite respect for a nation, of which we were the first individuals seen on these shores'. He was received by the Bey, who was in a mood of some insecurity, 'in doubt whether to expect the Tails or the bow-string'. He seemed, writes Beaufort, 'to imagine that I had a *firman* in my pocket for his deposition, and every time I moved, significant looks were exchanged between him and his attendants'. He could 'scarcely repress his joy when the day of our departure was announced'.

At this period, and indeed until modern times, the population of Adalia was one-third Greek. But the Greeks knew only Turkish, and were for the most part ignorant of the meaning of the Greek liturgy, which their priests recited. Fellows stayed with a Greek banker, who was far richer than the Pasha and lived in a 'perfect palace', served by Arab slaves who had cost him £6 or £8 apiece. 'Every house', he wrote, 'has its garden, and consequently the town has the appearance of a wood—and of what? Orange, lemon, fig, vine and mulberry, all cultivated with the artificial care of a town garden, and now in fresh spring beauty.'[1] Today there are no Greeks in Antalya, and the gardens of the houses, within the crumbling city walls, huddled closely together along tortuous cobbled streets, have an unkempt appearance.

Outside the walls, however, there is a long double Atatürk Boulevard, lined with acacias and leading proudly to an immense municipal garden, the Inönü Park. Built over the ancient bastions, commanding the sea, this is the creation of a *Vali* who once visited Vienna, saw the Prater, remembered what he could of it, and determined that the citizens of Antalya should enjoy a similar amenity. Similar in scale it certainly is, since it must be large enough to accommodate the citizens of Vienna in comfort. But it is a trifle too large for the mere twenty thousand inhabitants of Antalya. Keeping nature at bay with a pitiless expanse of concrete, it boasts avenues so broad that no trees can shade them, pergolas so vast that no creepers can cover them. In these wide-open spaces, scorched by the sunlight, the flowers strive valiantly to show off their blooms. In so far as they fail, they are amply supplemented in caricature by lamp-standards of ingenious floral designs—giant bluebells and mushrooms and trees of metal, with concrete stalks and trunks, all blooming at night with clusters of bright electric lamps. The solitude of the place is relieved here and there by groups of women who squat beneath the stunted palm-trees, plucking a weed which serves them as a form of spinach.

Beyond the great esplanade, decently hidden from sight, nature romps unchecked over the rich red earth down to the harbour, and here, amid a tangle of oak and olive, I found it possible to sit at ease and in the shade, contemplating a bay in which mountains and sea had achieved a serene and immaculate harmony. The sea was a coat without seam, woven of watered silk, its surface reflecting each nuance of sunlight, each shadow of a cloud, each flicker of a breeze, and transmuting them into an abstract pattern of the purest light and colour.

It was a surface apparently inviolate to the prow of a steamer, now gliding across it in a slow eddy of quicksilver, while the wake of boats, skimming out like suitors to woo her, left barely a ripple in their silken wake. Soaring up from it in folds of a velvet texture, catching and echoing the steamer's triple call, was the operatic silhouette of the mountain range which the ancients called Mount Climax. Well-named, it is a flight of Gothic peaks, stylized in form, poetic in line, mounting

[1] Sir Charles Fellows. *Travels and Researches in Asia Minor*. London: 1852.

in tiers to the sculptural climax of a summit which the Turks call the Çalbali Dağ. Distilled in this luminous formal panorama is the essential Mediterranean, Romantic and classical in one.

Embraced by this dramatic setting, given life by the myriad cascades, the Katarrhactes, which gush around it over the honey-combed rust-gold cliffs into the sea, lies the harbour of Antalya. It was still picturesque when first I saw it, contained in a crescent of dolls' house architecture, with the bluff city walls rising steeply above it amid rambling fig-trees and planes as tall as the cliffs themselves. Now it was growing functional, a place no longer to live in but to work in. The dolls' houses, one by one, were vanishing, to make room for a streamlined warehouse and larger quays, now stacked with chrome from the mountains. A pair of cube-like concrete shops barred the view between a vine-wreathed café and the sea. When I condoled with the proprietor, he said, with a dissatisfied shrug at his own timbered façade: 'They are good. They are modern.'

At night, when the quays must once have hummed with Greek tavern life, all was now dark and silent, but for the barking of a dog, the wail of Turkish radio music, the call to prayer from a miniature mosque, built apparently of cardboard, with a toy minaret. Through its lighted windows two sailors in skull-caps performed their devotions like figures in some gymnastic ballet. Otherwise life, in Antalya, had turned its back on the sea.

Inland moreover it had little to offer. There was no restaurant, only a murky 'dive' where lorry-drivers drank *raki*, but where it was possible to get *köfte* and wine flavoured with sea-water. It was small consolation that classical authors thought this to be good for the digestion. 'Wines', wrote Athenaeus, 'which are more carefully treated with sea-water, do not cause headache; they loosen the bowels, excite the stomach, cause inflations and assist digestion.' [1] He was referring to those of 'the brine-drinking people' of Myndus and Halicarnassus, in Caria. Pliny,[2] on the other hand, found the Ephesian wines 'unwholesome because seasoned with sea-water and boiled must'. The wine of Cilicia, says Athenaeus, was merely a laxative.

* * *

Adalia was founded, as Attaleia, in the second century B.C., by Attalus Philadelphus, King of Pergamum, whose dynasty dominated a large

[1] Athenaeus. *Deipnosophists*. Book I. [2] *Natural History*. Book XIV.

part of western Asia Minor, and was in early alliance with the Romans. It seems to have been the youngest of a group of cities which profited by the fertility of the Pamphylian plain, with its two great rivers, the Cestrus and the Eurymedon, and which had been colonized at various times by the Greeks. Attaleia flourished, above all of them, in Roman times, as St. Paul and St. Barnabas must have found when they embarked here for Antioch, and amid the ruins of its walls is a triple Roman gateway dedicated to Hadrian. Its prosperity continued into the Byzantine Age, and there survives as a museum a substantial church, which the Seljuks converted into a mosque, using Byzantine columns to build a gateway, and adding a fluted brick minaret. Even until the eighteenth century a superstition lingered that the Christians would recapture the town, and the gates were closed 'each Friday between twelve and one, the time at which this was expected to happen'.[1] The walls survived until late in the nineteenth century, when they were largely pulled down by the Turks themselves.

Three earlier cities lie to the east of it, strung out along a plain which is a modest strip of land compared to the deep broad acres of Cilicia. Asiatic perhaps in origin, they were Hellenized at some time during the first millennium B.C. but spoke a language which, like that of Soli, was a mixture of Greek and native forms.[2] The first is Perge, the Perga in Pamphylia where St. Paul and St. Barnabas landed on their arrival from Cyprus.[3] They sailed up the Cestrus which, as the Aksu, has ceased to be navigable owing to the accumulation of silt from the Taurus. It was an important city in Roman times, and its ruins are a wilderness of Roman stone, amid a devouring tumult of sweet-scented trees. The drum-like masonry of a Roman theatre rises above the chaos, its cumbrous arcades overlooking a stadium which once held an audience of twelve thousand people. A single Turkish peasant now occupied it, planting the arena with cotton and stabling his cattle in the vaults beneath the seats.

In the north wind, blowing from beyond the Taurus, the landscape rang with light. The mountains, their heads lightly powdered with snow, their loins drenched in a deep blue shadow, stood forward in sharp relief. From a clothing of pine-forest they thrust out crags, all levelled and cleared as though demanding that cities be built on them;

[1] Paul Lucas. *Voyage dans la Grèce et l'Asie Mineure*. Amsterdam: 1714.
[2] David Magie. *Roman Rule in Asia Minor*. Princeton: 1950.
[3] Acts of the Apostles xiii. 13.

and on one stands the acropolis of Aspendus. A Roman aqueduct, bold as a railway viaduct, strides towards it from the mountains across the valley of the Eurymedon,[1] a luminous ribbon of blue. Commanding the river, from the base of the hill, is a building so massive and severe that from a distance it has the aspect of a factory. A skyscraper, seven storeys high, it is a Roman theatre, surviving all but intact. The entrance front is austerely functional, unrelieved by ornament; within, the proscenium rises to the full height of the building, elaborate as some façade of the Renaissance, its ranks of columns and pediments framing niches from which only the statues are missing, some pillaged, it seems, by the Romans themselves. The central pediment is carved with an effigy of Bacchus, wrongly supposed by the Turks to be a female, hence called Bal Kiz, the 'Honey Girl', the name which the place now bears. Four flights of stairs lead to the top of the theatre, which has forty tiers of seats and, encircling the auditorium, two broad, vaulted foyers, of which one has arcades looking on to the scene. Today, in the summer, the Turks now use the theatre for periodic performances of Shakespeare in Turkish, or bouts of wrestling, their favourite sport. In its ponderous scale, palatial decor, and competent construction, it epitomizes *Pax Romana* in all its solid colonial efficiency.

In the more restless days of the Greeks, Aspendus claimed to have been founded by the Argives, who were then able to sail their ships right up the Eurymedon to the walls of the city. The colonists, whoever they may have been, traded successfully in salt, oil and wool and their coinage had wide circulation. They also bred horses for the Persian kings. The Eurymedon and its neighbourhood were the scene of two key naval battles, the first sealing Greek, the second Roman supremacy. In 469 B.C. a large Athenian fleet sailed up the river, under Cimon, to pursue and defeat the Persians, while his soldiers defeated them on land. Thus, 'like a well-trained athelete at the games', he 'carried off two victories in one day, surpassing that of Salamis by sea, and that of Plataea by land'.[2] On a later naval occasion Alcibiades had come here, persuading the Persian Tissaphernes to send home the pro-Spartan fleet of the Phoenicians. Later Aspendus tried to buy off Alexander, but, deceiving him, was subdued, and that was the end of its independence.

An awkward neighbour of Aspendus was the lawless city of Side,

[1] Now the Köprü Irmak.

[2] Plutarch. *Life of Cimon.*

originally claimed to have been a colony of the Aeolians. This was the site of the second great battle, in 190 B.C., when a Roman fleet, supported by Rhodians, defeated that of Antiochus, with Hannibal on board. The marble ruins of Side lie strewn over a promontory below the Turkish village of Manavgat, where I rested for an hour in a café beneath spreading plane-trees, by the swift smooth waters of the Melas. Endowed with a natural double harbour, Side developed a tough seafaring tradition. It became an arsenal of the Cilician pirates, who built their ships here, while Coracesium (now Alanya), to the East, was their principal fortress. The pirates used to sell their prisoners as slaves by public auction, though they admitted them to be freemen,[1] and the tradition persisted, though in a more orthodox form, under the Romans, who built up Side into an important slave-market. The 'quasi-Semitic' dialect and coinage of Side suggest that the city was not properly a Greek one.[2] In Byzantine times it was settled by Jews.

Today it is settled sparsely by Cretans, who graze their herds among the broken columns and pedestals of the slave-market, an arcaded *agora* of imposing size. The substantial Roman theatre, with little high ground to enfold it, is built up on a semicircular vaulted arcade which served as a shopping street, and indeed today recalls some street in modern Rome. Here the Cretans showed me a spot where foreign excavators, or so they alleged, had unearthed a bag of gold and, instead of sharing it out, had quietly absconded with it in the night—doubtless an apocryphal tale such as is freely told by the oriental peasant to the discredit of the western archaeologist. Camped on a smooth white beach among pine-trees, archaeologists were still working on the ruins of a temple. Throughout the city there are signs of an elaborate system of irrigation, which must have cooled the streets and markets, a noble monument to the engineers of the Roman P.W.D.

* * *

Before leaving Antalya I climbed up into the cluster of Gothic peaks which presides so romantically over its bay. The bus left me at a roadside coffee-house, near the head of the pass which leads from Pamphylia into Pisidia. It is a gateway commanded on either side by precipitous crags, which has often proved impregnable and would have defeated Alexander had not the Pisidians retired at night to their homes, leaving only a small force to guard it. He passed through nevertheless, on his

[1] Strabo. *Geography*. Book XIV.

[2] Magie. *op. cit.*

way up into Phrygia, without besieging their rock-bound city of Termessus. These Pisidians were a tough barbarian race, who gave the Romans much trouble from their mountain strongholds, in alliance with the pirates on the coast. Their subjugation set the seal on *Pax Romana*, with its colonial development, and the pass became a royal road, open to all.

A century earlier the Romans had subdued and modernized Termessus, which crowns the flat top of a ridge, dominating the sea on the one hand and an inland valley on the other. Already on the road I had passed the towers and walls of its pre-Roman fortifications. Now, escorted by a guide and his friend from the roadside coffee-house, I climbed the stony path which leads towards the city itself, through an aromatic wilderness of arbutus and myrtle and bay. Fresh green pines gave an air of youth to the rugged landscape, while the leaves of oaks made a pattern against deep gold limestone cliffs. The Turks call this Güllük Dağ, the Rose Mountain, and in season it is sweet with wild roses. After half an hour's climb we began to reach the outskirts of the city: the trace of a gateway, tombs hewn from the rock, marble sarcophagi carved in relief. One was the tomb of a horseman, adorned with shield and spear and horse's head; another that of a hoplite, his recumbent effigy thrown into sharp relief by the sunlight. Here was the head of a lion, there a boat, with an heraldic fish.

But the city is so large that it was nearly an hour before we reached its centre, an imposing mass of public buildings, including two Doric ruins, a Roman palace and an *agora*, with elaborate vaulted cisterns beneath it. It held water still, which we drank, kneeling on the drum of a broken Roman column. Climbing farther, we finally emerged on the summit of the ridge, a commanding strategic point where it would have been natural to find a fortress. But since this was *Pax Romana* we found, instead, a Roman theatre, one of the loftiest and most dramatic in the classical world. The stage stands poised on the brink of an abyss, reinforced by the walls and buttresses of expert Roman engineers. The auditorium looks across it to a grandiose natural spectacle, a backcloth and wings which are the summit of a mountain and a perspective of spurs and pinnacles. A great crag like a battle-axe cleaves the sky; a great ridge like the blade of a scimitar curves sharply away from it down into a remote still sea, shining below. It was a scene which wore its majesty lightly, ever-changing and serene.

With an embracing gesture my guide explained:

'*Sinama*.'

'Yes,' I said. 'Cinema.'

'Who built it?' he asked.

'The Romans, two thousand years ago.'

'What became of them?'

'They became the Italians.'

'The Italians!' He made an exclamation of scorn. The Italians were not popular when they occupied Antalya between 1918 and 1922.

We got back to the road two minutes after the bus to Antalya had gone. Here a curious figure had attracted attention, a talkative Italian, with a green bicycle and an umbrella, who informed me that he was on his way to Rome. The Turks looked at him in expressionless silence as he went his way, pushing his bicycle up the hillside in the gathering dusk. For some hours I waited in the coffee-house, hoping that a lorry would pass. Darkness fell. A gendarme and a forester drank coffee in silence, warming themselves at a stove which they fed with frequent logs. On a wooden divan, strewn with skins and straw matting, an old man prayed as though to his shadow, flung on the wall, gently swaying, by an acetylene lamp. Then he took off his socks and warmed grimy white feet at a cooker where chicken-broth was simmering. A boy was cutting up fresh goats' meat, piling lean on one dish, fat on another, then threading pieces alternately together on spits, for *kebabs*. Drugged by the smells of the smoke and the meat and the feet, I lay and dozed on the hard divan, resigned to spending the night on it, beneath the glare of the acetylene lamp. But late in the evening a lorry appeared, and I drove back to Antalya beneath a moon which tamed the landscape into a scented park, throwing soft pine shadows across the earth.

CHAPTER 4

LYCIA (I)

A Leisurely Voyage—The Land of the Chimaera—Phaselis and Olympus—Finike and its future—Land against Sea—Myra and its Cemetery—The Legends of St. Nicholas

I LEFT ANTALYA in the company of my friend David Balfour, the British Consul-General in Izmir, sailing westwards in his motor-yacht whimsically named, by a previous owner, the *Elfin*. We were bent on a voyage in the style of consuls more past than present, a leisurely inspection of the Turkish coastlands, showing the British flag. *Elfin* was a small craft with room for two passengers, a cook and a navigator, and we had time and repose and an endless procession of sunlit seascapes ahead of us. As we weighed anchor the master of a caique alongside us was laboriously painting her name on the bows, TÜRKGÜCU, ANTALYA, in Roman script, but from right to left, in Arabic style.

From the harbour mouth the honey-coloured cliffs looked soft as rock cake, crumbled by the cataracts, baked by the sun. As we sailed across the bay the silhouette of Mount Climax came slowly into focus, revealing forests of pine-trees, sweet rough hillsides, limestone cliffs all stained and streaked like a giant painter's palette. By an island, flung out like a nugget into the clear green water, we relished our first bathe. Beside us a cormorant dived busily for fish; above us seagulls planed looking for it with querulous cries, incapable of graceless movement. Where these cliffs slope steeply down to the sea a road was now being built. Alexander's army had to take a circuitous route through the mountains, but Alexander himself, with a few of his closest followers, waded waist-deep through the waves.[1] Since a storm was blowing this was clearly a risky operation, though Arrian's version suggests that only a change in the wind made it possible.[2] Callisthenes chose to

[1] Strabo. *Geography*. Book XIV. [2] Arrian. *Anabasis*. Book I.

attribute its success to the fact that the sea abased its waters, in homage to Alexander as King. The road comes to an end at the village of Kemer—a name taken presumably from the Chimaera, the 'unceasing flame' [1] of classical legend, which lies in the hills, some twenty miles to the south of it. Beaufort visited it, and reports that it is like an oven, a small volcanic crater where the Turkish shepherds cooked their food and declared that it would not roast stolen meat. Spratt and Forbes found two old Turks there, with two black slaves, who had come to get some of its soot, valued as remedy for sore eyelids and a dye for the eyebrows.[2]

As we cruised on southwards, lazing in the sunshine, the pine-forests thickened, the landscape grew wilder and emptier. Presently there came into view, beneath the wooded slopes, a city of evident size. We glided into a small but well-built harbour, with substantial quays and breakwaters. But there was not a soul to be seen. For this was a Roman city and a Roman harbour, the city of Phaselis, uninhabited for a thousand years and more. Its earliest builders, Dorian colonists, chose a fine site for it, the smooth, flat neck of a rocky peninsula with a natural harbour on either side. A straight Roman street, still largely paved with stone, leads across it from one harbour to the other. Walls of its houses and plinths of its statues survive on either side amid a tangle of pine and myrtle, and a shallow stairway leads down to the shingly white beach beyond. Roman stones are strewn over it, some carved and inscribed, and among them I came upon a dead flying-fish, blue-winged as a swallow. Nearby a pier has been built from the plinths of statues, their inscriptions still visible beneath the sea.

Here we lingered in solitude, enjoying a landscape soft and luxuriant beneath a sun which shone down unrestrained over the mountains. Beyond the harbour a striped shadowed rock rose high from the sea; before us a rich broad valley swept up through the forests towards the airy grey dome of Mount Solyma, now the Tahtali Dağ. To the south of it is Musa Dağ, a mountain supposedly visited by Moses on his flight from Egypt. Beaufort suggests here a confusion with Mount Horeb, the Chimaera being mistaken in legend for the Burning Bush. Solyma is a mountain where roses bloom profusely, so that in classical times the attar of roses of Phaselis was compared with that of Naples and

[1] Pliny. *Natural History*. Book II.

[2] Lt. T. A. B. Spratt and Prof. Edward Forbes. *Travels in Lycia*. London: 1847.

Capua.[1] It is a mountain also of disturbing habits. Beaufort was told that 'every autumn a mighty groan is heard to issue from the summit of the mountain, louder than the report of any cannon, but unaccompanied by fire or smoke' and that this was 'an annual summons to the Elect to make the best of their way to Paradise'.

Phaselis has a third harbour, at the outlet of a lake, now a noisome swamp which even in the time of Livy and Cicero was renowned for its 'baneful exhalations', making the place unhealthy. An aqueduct, solidly built, with the relics of broad Roman arches, leads towards it and must once have crossed its mouth. Nearby a pier has been built from the plinths of statues, their inscriptions still visible beneath the sea, and the woods around conceal a necropolis which, from the evidence of a sarcophagus lately broken, local fishermen still think worthy of robbery. The main part of the city was built on the higher ground, at the head of the peninsula. Here the cliff has fallen away, and as we coasted along it we saw, revealed in section, the shafts of Roman wells, sunk into the ground from the houses above. Cut off from the land by its mountains, Phaselis was clearly the city of a maritime power and indeed it was for long an important pirate base. It was in this region that the Romans finally disposed of the pirate chieftain Zenicetus, who, seeing himself beaten, set fire to most of Phaselis and flung himself, with his family and friends, into the flames. When finally Pompey came to Phaselis, mopping up the pirates, he found it almost deserted. The city survived from Roman into Byzantine times and the more roughly built Byzantine walls show signs of fortifications, scarred by battles against the invading Saracens.

Sailing gently down this coast, it was hard to sympathize with Fellows who wrote, as he reluctantly did so, hankering for the land: 'I have ever become insensible to the monotony of a (sea) voyage, as compared with other travel, and continually long for its termination.' Phaselis, he complained in this mood, was small: 'In the same degree in which the ruins of the cities in the interior have raised my conception of the grandeur, both in scale, design, and execution, of the works of the ancients, the vestiges of their ports and harbours diminish my idea of their naval strength and skill.' The city had seemed to us monumental, the harbour indestructible. Now towards evening, as the shadows softened the contours of the lonely wooded coast-line, we drew into a cove where a natural garden glowed pink by the sands of a

[1] Athenaeus. *Deipnosophists*. Book XV.

clean white beach. Groves of oleanders were blooming in abundance, by the banks of a stream running diagonally across the shingle to the sea, and from among them arose the walls of yet another ruined city, Olympus. Strabo names it as one of the six largest cities of the Lycians, which they chose for security to build in inaccessible places, and of which all today are deserted and forgotten.[1] They were a people who, unlike the piratical Cilicians, 'continued to live as good citizens and with so much restraint upon themselves, that although the Pamphylians had succeeded in obtaining the sovereignty of the sea as far as Italy, yet they were never influenced by the desire of base gain, and persevered in administering the affairs of the state according to the laws of the Lycian body'. Herodotus [2] believes that the Lycians were not a people indigenous to Asia Minor, but that they came from Crete—a theory not supported by modern scholars. Sung by Homer, they were prominent allies of Troy, lending their warriors, like Sarpedon and Pandarus, to fight in the Trojan War, honouring Trojan gods and heroes, like Apollo and Bellerophon, giving Trojan names, like Xanthus and Tlos, to their rivers and cities. A nation of consequence, they refused to submit to the Persians, and had to be subdued by force. Their city of Olympus eventually declined into a haunt of the pirates.

In the balmy scented evening air, we wandered by the banks of its white-bedded stream. As befits a river in a city it was still solidly walled, at first with smooth-faced Roman stones, then higher up, beyond the ruins of a Roman bridge, with rougher Byzantine stone, unfaced, between courses of brick. The opposite hillside was decorated at intervals with pillared classical tombs, and with a fringe of Byzantine battlements. On a point, perched boldly above the sea, was a toy Genoese castle, its ramparts incorporating a miniature arch, skilfully bridging a headlong cleft in the rock. Amid the tangle of myrtle and well-grown bay-trees rampaging over the site of the city, we came upon the ruins of a Byzantine chapel or tomb, then scrambled onwards to find a tall rectangular gateway, Greek or Roman, rising above the tops of the trees. It should have led to a temple, but led curiously nowhere, merely to the edge of a swamp, like that of Phaselis. Nor, though Beaufort refers to the remains of a temple, were any to be seen, in or around its stagnant waters.

Soon dusk began to fall over the fragrant oleanders, the weathered stones, the swift-running, solitary stream. We left Olympus with

[1] *Geography*. Book XIV. [2] *History*. Book VII.

regret, unlike Fellows, who found it even smaller than Phaselis, and on a later visit confessed himself 'disappointed at finding himself in a place I cared little to see again'. Meanwhile he writes 'I was rejoiced to resume my travels on *terra firma*' and he had no sooner done so 'than objects of interest appeared'. We sailed on for a while, through the gentle undulations of a sea growing dark as wine in the sunset, then anchored for the night, as mediaeval barques must have done, in Porto Genovese, a natural harbour, between high sheltering cliffs, like some secret land-locked fjord.

The Turkish name for Olympus is Deliktaş, the 'Perforated Rock'. For, behind the city, a narrow cleft in the rock makes a passage through towards the shores of the Gulf of Finike. We reached it next morning by a more circuitous route, rounding Cape Chelidonia, the 'Sacred Promontory', with its precipitous, satellite islands which Strabo compares to the 'skirt of a mountain'. It was here, in the view of the ancients, that the Taurus began, a range which was held to traverse, under different names, the whole continent of Asia.[1] Beyond the cape the range sweeps back in folds from the coast, making way for a river and for an alluvial plain, like that of Pamphylia. Here the land is bound to the sea by an arc of dull gold sand and a fringe of palm-trees. Along the beach a file of camels marched, loaded with firewood, contrasting with a bright red tractor which lumbered across the cotton-fields behind. The soil was being reclaimed by modern methods of irrigation, and the farmers were beginning to prosper. But the cultivation of rice was curtailed, since its flooded fields had for long afflicted the plain with malaria, a curse from which its people were only now recovering. Finike, their port, at the western end of the bay, is still a mere street of unplastered houses with a few poor shops. On the one hand the river coils slowly to the sea, green weeds trailing to and fro, like lustrous tresses, beneath its surface; on the other the mountains encroach once more, tumbling down on the village in a rugged stairway of boulders, permitting no vegetation but a desiccated scrub. Here, with a view to Finike's more prosperous future, stone was being quarried from the hillside and flung into the sea, to make the foundations of a new jetty.

With a porpoise close before us cavorting lazily through the waves, we glided westwards along the coast. The occasional shimmer of a flight of birds threw an undulating curtain across the hillside. Light clouds cast shadows down over the mountains, blue as the sea itself.

[1] Pliny. *Natural History*. Book V.

Presently a long white sandbank stretched before us, the shingly strand of Demre. Here, in eternal conflict, sea and river pile up land to the enrichment of the plain between them. The shingle makes a wall to keep the river from the sea; the river, as it thrusts and curves to find an outlet, leaves valuable silt behind it; and the benefactor is man. Beyond the bay of Demre, behind a promontory sheltering the classical port of Andriace, where Brutus once anchored and St. Paul transhipped, we anchored for a leisurely bathe in the green translucent water. It had grown so shallow, over the centuries, that we were soon wading knee-deep, towards a shore still distant. The sea was warm beneath, but cold on the surface, from the current of a brackish stream which had found a way out to it. Its water tasted more fresh than salt but with a tart, sulphuric flavour. On the beach, hemmed in by the sand, was an overflow of the stream, a stagnant pool of livid green. Venturing into it, I found it as warm as a bath and lay back in its uninviting waters happily soaking. The Consul-General meanwhile was spearing bright blue crabs, which abounded in the sandy shallows. They seemed large, and we looked forward to a meal of them in the evening. But, when cooked, they shrank to a mere few mouthfuls and we were glad of a more substantial silver fish, the only catch of a passing fisherman.

Meanwhile we wandered inland in the stillness of the afternoon heat, exploring the overgrown Byzantine city which straggles along the banks of the stream. At the northern end of it, facing inland, is a wall put roughly together from a jumble of Roman and Byzantine stones and column-drums, evidently in hurried defence against the threat of the Saracen invader. Across the narrowing stream the land has won its battle against the sea, converting a navigable gulf into a marsh, now drying with a faint, familiar smell of drains. On the edge of it stood a long pedimented building of well-faced stone, like some handsome Georgian Customs House. It was a Roman grain store built by Hadrian for his Navy, its cornice incisively carved, from one end to the other, with an inscription in his honour. Beaufort found two busts, presumably of Hadrian and his wife, in its walls, but they have now disappeared. The source of the stream nearby has been given the vaulted dignity of a Roman bath-house where the Roman sailors must have bathed and taken the sulphurous waters. Their flavour attracted large fish to the river of Andriace and at a fountain of Apollo in these regions the fish, responding to a triple call on the flute, foretold the future. If they ate the food which was thrown to them the omens were good; if they rejected it with their tails the omens were bad.[1] Today, a former Turkish sailor has erected a mill-wheel by the stream, to grind the wheat which grows on the reclaimed land.

Drugged with heat, we moved with slow tentative strides across the dried-up stubble towards the village of Demre which stands below the hill. We passed the roof of a Lycian tomb, projecting above the earth which had buried it. On the outskirts of the village was a well, so precious as to be barrel-vaulted, like a chapel. A stripling plane-tree, planted in front of it, was being carefully nurtured with a brushwood fence, to shade future generations. The village well was shaded with older, nobler trees. In a café beneath a mulberry's spreading branches, we drank glass after glass of lemonade, freshly pressed from the fruit of the citrus groves around, and cooled, not by ice, but by handfuls of snow from the Taurus peaks. Each day a peasant rode far up to a sunless, hence perennial northern snowdrift, to collect two sacks of it and ride back through the night, six hours each way. Such was his living.

A dreamlike paralysis silenced the village 'square', whose insubstantial houses gave it the air of a stage. An occasional figure moved across it in laborious slow motion: a man on a camel, craning its neck to snap at the upper branches of a tree; a small boy on a donkey, carrying a large black umbrella. Villagers huddled around us, motionless in the shade. They were Turks from Macedonia, exchanged for the Greeks who had for centuries inhabited Demre. Two, fairer than the rest, had a smile for us, and an alert curiosity, betraying Greek affiliations; two others were black as Africans, lanky, expressionless, torpid. No longer were they ravaged by smallpox, as in the days of Texier; [2] no longer, as in the days of Fellows, did plagues of gnats drive them into the mountains, throughout the summer months. The place was now reasonably healthy, and moreover growing more prosperous. The villagers were content. The Democrat Government had remitted their taxes and showered them with loans; some day the loans must be repaid, but 'Money,' they shrewdly said, 'brings money'. Thanks to new walls and a new road, they were growing and exporting more produce than ever in the past. The new wells abounded. The well-heads of two were smugly inscribed 'D.P.',[3] in the concrete; a third

[1] Pliny. [2] Charles Texier. *Asie Mineure*. Paris: 1862.
[3] Democrat Party.

had acquired a mechanical water-wheel, though it was still conservatively drawn by a bullock; another had been bored, more than fifty feet down, on the site of a Roman tomb, revealing Roman stones. Conduits sparkled away from it in all directions to fertilize fields where, for the first time, orange-trees grew.

Demre, as Myra, was the home of St. Nicholas—otherwise Santa Claus—the versatile patron saint of virgins, sailors, pawnbrokers and children—to say nothing of Imperial Russia. Nicholas gave three purses of gold, anonymously, to the three virgin daughters of an impoverished nobleman, at Patara nearby, to serve them as marriage dowries and so save them from a life of prostitution. Hence 'Christmas' stockings on the Eve of St. Nicholas—gifts transported, no longer on the back of his Mediterranean donkey, but by the more Nordic reindeer. Hence also the three golden balls—representing the three purses—of the pawnbroker. He is portrayed with these, and also with three boys in a tub—the three who were murdered by an inkeeper in Myra, cut up and concealed in tubs of brine, but put together and miraculously restored to life by St. Nicholas's prayers. The children revere him perhaps for this; the sailors—including the pirates—because he calmed the storms, and saved them from drowning, and gave them sound nautical advice about the tides and winds and rocks of this treacherous coast. Right up to modern times sailors, in search of his protection, were among the shrine's most profitable visitors.

St. Nicholas, who was born in Patara and became Bishop of Myra, lived in the time of Diocletian, and was duly persecuted for his Faith. His cult, which made his tomb here at Myra a centre of pilgrimage, became popular among the Greeks in the sixth century, when Justinian consecrated a church to him in Constantinople, and among the Latins three centuries later. The Saracens, on capturing Myra, tried to destroy his tomb, but the Greek Christians, to save their relics, led them astray, and they destroyed another instead. It was the Latin Christians who finally sacked it. A party of merchants from Bari, on the way home from Syria during the eleventh century, bribed the monks who were guarding it, broke it open, and made off with the relics. Their arrival in Bari caused a profound sensation throughout the Christian world, a church being built and a feast being inaugurated in honour of the Saint. Some Venetian merchants, thus outstripped but not to be outdone, returned to Venice, with some relics which they too pretended were those of St. Nicholas.[1] All that remained of the Saint was taken to St. Petersburg by a Russian frigate during the Greek War of Independence, and a gaudy picture sent in its place.[2] The museum at Antalya contains a gaudy picture of the Saint, and some relics which are claimed by the Turks to be his.

Former travellers lodged at the monastery, which adjoined the Church of St. Nicholas. The call to the evening service was sounded by a small boy hammering at a plank, since the Turks prohibited bells.[3] The monastery has disappeared, but the church survives, so engulfed by the advancing land that none of it now emerges above ground: only a bleak superstructure, of recent date, built on top of it. To enter the church we clambered down into the earth, by a rough stepped path. It is a lofty rectangular building, with two side-aisles, or baptisteries. The nave has been vaulted with brick in modern times, perhaps by the Russians, for whom it was a place of pilgrimage, but the structure embodies much that must date from Byzantium. There is no iconostasis, merely a group of four columns, Roman or Byzantine, a feature of the iconoclastic period; and behind them the seats have been built in the form of an amphitheatre, as in early Greek churches. Set into niches are two sarcophagi, of which one may be Byzantine. The other, which has been broken open, is incredibly stated to be that of St. Nicholas. Elaborately carved in the Roman manner and surmounted by two mutilated reclining figures, it is clearly a pagan classical tomb, unlikely to have been borrowed by a Christian community for the burial of its Bishop.[4] It may have been placed there, for some purpose, in the Middle Ages.

Classical remains abound at Myra, though much must be buried beneath the ground. By the road, through orchards of almond and citrus, which leads to the ancient city, are the ruins of elaborate Roman baths. They have been stripped down to their brickwork, but their facing stones have been used by the inhabitants to build a monumental wall, dividing their orchards from the roadside. Much must have been destroyed, if we are to believe Cockerell, who, as he was examining

[1] Texier. *op. cit.*

[2] Spratt and Forbes. *op. cit.*

[3] Spratt and Forbes. *op. cit.*

[4] Rex Miller (*In Search of Santa Claus*. Turkish Press, Broadcasting and Tourist Department) declares it to be 'apparently of later date than the church itself, probably a more elaborate replacement of the original fourth-century repository of the body of the saint'. He even suggests that the figures may be those of St. Nicholas and 'some youth or maiden of whom he was particularly fond'.

some statues, heard a Turk exclaim: 'If the infidels are attracted here by these blasphemous figures, the temptation shall soon cease; for when that dog is gone, I will destroy them.'[1] But the distinction of Myra lies in its multitude of tombs, carved, as at Petra, out of the living rock, hence less easily destroyed. Their rectangular façades, arrayed in regular terraces and storeys, impose architectural symmetry on the rough face of a precipice, which rises directly behind the Roman theatre. Standardized in design, golden in colour where the chisel has broken the weathered grey face of the limestone, they have been carved by the Lycians in exact imitation of wooden doorways, with pillars, projecting cornices like beams, and oblong panels, enclosed by mullions. Where a panel has been broken the effect is that of a safe which has been burgled. Many have pediments, in the Roman manner, together with inscriptions in the Lycian dialect, Roman and Greek. Texier found a touching inscription, scratched on the wall of a tomb, perhaps with the ferrule of a Greek shepherd's crook: 'Moschus loves Philiste, the daughter of Demetrius'. Carved on the cliff-face itself are some bas-reliefs in the Roman manner, representing gods or heroes.

This vertical cemetery dominates the auditorium of the theatre, creating a nice classical harmony between living and dead. Today it was planted with a crop of sweet ripe tomatoes: a theatre of imposing size, with massive archways and vaulted corridors and the relics of a pillared proscenium. As we left it a fierce dog bared its teeth, preparing to attack us. Its owner, with apparent reluctance, called it off, gazing after us with a surly look. In the evening light, between the setting of the sun and the rising of the moon, we walked back with a sprightlier step through the fields, until the sweet smell of the harvest, reaped and garnered, gave place to the sulphurous reek of the marsh. The walls of the Byzantine city, by the banks of the stream, shone white as walls of marble in the rising softening moonlight, giving it the air of a city inhabited but sleeping. Taking a warm bath in the stagnant pool, on the beach, we ran, then swam through the cooling sea, back to the lamplit cabin of the *Elfin*.

[1] Quoted by Beaufort. *op. cit.*

CHAPTER 5

LYCIA (2)

The Lycian Dead—Andifli and Castelorizo—Death of a Greek Island?—Arrest at Patara—The Seven Capes—Progress reaches Fethiye—Telmessus

EARLY NEXT MORNING we sailed into the narrow roadstead of Tristomon, a three-headed isthmus with two small harbours, secreted behind the long humped island of Kakava. A miniature Genoese fort, nicely perched on a spur, points the way inwards, and presently a castle emerges, its battlements, alternately Genoese and Turkish, encircling a bald pate of rock. Within its walls are the ruins of a small Roman theatre, and all around it Roman stones give dignity to quays and walls and houses. Among fig trees and olives and wild delphinium, a Turkish village scrambles down haphazard to the quay. Climbing upwards in the heat, which already paralysed the landscape, I found it entirely deserted; the population had taken to the fields, where they were gathering in the harvest.

Only the Lycian dead watched over Tristomon, their tombs silhouetted like sentry-boxes along the rocky skyline. Here was the classic Lycian tomb, not hewn from the rock, as at Myra, but standing up straight and tall, built solidly of stone, in permanent imitation of the more transient timbered arks which still serve as grain-stores in the surrounding Turkish villages. Each wooden beam has been faithfully reproduced in stone, supporting a roof like that of a penthouse which slopes steeply upwards or, more elegantly, curves to a point in the ogival manner. These monumental dwellings of the ancient dead seem to have grown back into the rocks on which they stand, their man-hewn steps so worn and weathered, so wrapped around with organic matter that they have become one with the stones of the earth. One has toppled on its side, a Cyclopean ruin. Another below has been engulfed by the sea, its roof emerging above it like the crown of a reef.

From the top of the castle I looked down over a stretch of red earth and stubble, fringing the inner harbour, a few fields which the stony landscape has yielded to the villagers. Here, like figures in a Breughel landscape, they were stacking the grain; and here too, preserving continuity, the dead—their own, more familiar Moslem dead—watched over them. For the fields were also cemeteries, where families camped and worked and slept among the whitewashed tombs of the Faithful.

We sailed westwards away from the deserted roadstead, beneath the walls of a second Genoese fort, twin of the first. There was no sign of life on Kakava, the Island (in Greek) of the Partridges, where Beaufort describes an abandoned village and a small Christian chapel, visited by Greek sailors to practise their devotions with no Turks to molest them. He was, for the present, over-optimistic in his conclusion that 'future events may possibly restore this place to its former population and importance . . . its great extent, its bold shores, and the facility of defence, may hereafter point it out as an eligible place for the rendezvous of a fleet'. Nevertheless a Turkish submarine was able to hide here from the Allies during the First World War, an exploit commemorated by the Turkish star and crescent and an appropriate inscription, traced on the surface of a rock.

Kaş, our next port of call, lies on a blue silken bay, beneath folds of rose-coloured mountains. Otherwise Andifli, the Antiphellus of Strabo, we found it as torpid as Demre, a port drained of the life which the Greeks once brought to it. On the one hand a tall Lycian tomb stands sentry over the village; on the other an abandoned Greek church, its interior painted a garish blue and white. Its aisles were now stacked with drums of petrol, and a pair of doves nested quietly in the eaves above its altar. Beyond it, carved out of the hillside, a small Hellenistic theatre looks out to sea; beneath it the relics of an *agora*. Over the ridge more tombs, of an imposing character, Lycian and Roman, look down on a second harbour, more secret even than that of Tristomon, where British ships used to hide during the Second World War. The village, with its whitewashed houses and fretted balconies, and its cobbled square shaded by aged planes, betrays Greek influence. But today it has an unkempt, careless look.

Fellows describes Andifli as 'an active little trading harbour for firewood'. It is a place which still depends for its living on the timber of the mountainsides, and the office of the mayor smelt sweetly of cedar-wood panelling, flavoured with D.D.T. The *Kaymakam*, whom we visited in a larger but more ramshackle office, furnished with well-worn leather armchairs and a faded photograph of Atatürk, assured us that the trade still flourished, especially in valona oak, which is used in the tanning trade. The new government, he added, had built a road inland which encouraged it; moreover caiques still came into Kaş now and then, to carry cedar-wood to Egypt. But the activity of the harbour is not what it once was. It depended on the island of Megiste, in Turkish Meis, in Italian Castelrosso, in modern Greek Castelorizo, two-and-a-half miles across the sound—once 'the most important place on the coasts, the residence of European consuls',[1] whose Greek inhabitants, shipbuilders and traders, carried the timber trade in partnership with the Greeks on the mainland, and indeed had a hand in the trade of all the south-west coast. As a part of Turkey, Castelorizo was the capital of a province, with a population of up to twenty thousand Greeks. Between the two world wars, under Italian rule, this dwindled to six thousand; today, under Greek rule, it is little more than six hundred. The *Kaymakam* barked out a laugh when we asked after his Greek island neighbours.

'We don't see much of them,' he said, 'except that they're always poaching fish in our waters. Sometimes they come over to steal. They're glad of a night or two in a Turkish prison, with decent meals.'

Otherwise a curtain has descended between the Turkish mainland and this remote outpost of Greece, sixty miles from the nearest Greek island,[2] three-hundred-and-fifty from Athens. As a concession we were allowed to penetrate the curtain: to sail across to Castelorizo and back again. Normal customs regulations would have obliged us, on leaving it, to return to some larger Turkish port. It was a bare enough shore which greeted us, a red waterless hillside with the relics of a fort, which must have inspired the Genoese name of Castel Rosso; a few niggardly strips of stubble, wrested from the rock. Through the heat of the afternoon, when all Greeks sleep, we lay at anchor in a sheltered bay, exploring a deserted whitewashed chapel and the ruins of a concrete pill-box, enjoying our first Greek bathe, in luminous waters, from white rocks baked by the sun. Later two Greek boys, curly headed and bronzed, swam out to the *Elfin*, sent to ask whether we had missed the harbour entrance. Taking pleasure in the exercise of his fluent Greek speech, the Consul-General explained that we were

[1] Fellows. *op. cit.* [2] Rhodes.

merely awaiting the cool of the evening. They swam swiftly off, and as the sun fell we sailed into port.

Coming suddenly into view around a headland, built closely along three sides of a neat square harbour, the town looked at us from symmetrical, wide-open windows, with an aliveness essentially Greek. Here, as we landed, was no lassitude, but a vigorous curiosity. Where had we come from? Where were we going? Who indeed were we? Two brisk Greek gendarmes, taut in their uniforms, walked us up through the steep paved streets of the town, all house-proud and street-proud, shaded by vines, each house with a bright painted balcony and a whitewashed doorstep. At the top, looking down over the serene glassy sea and a cluster of gold rocks resting upon it, stood an ample white church, spick and span, its courtyards carpeted with pebble mosaic in ingenious geometrical patterns, its vaulted nave flanked by Corinthian columns from the temple of Apollo at Patara. During the war, we were told, the Germans and Italians tried to remove these columns, the pride of the island, but all the citizens assembled in an indignant mob to prevent them. The church had been well restored in the nineteenth century, during the period of the island's prosperity, and a school had been built, in the Greek classical manner, beside it. But a second school, given by an Alexandrine Greek, with busts of himself and his wife to adorn it, remained incomplete, perhaps a monument to the fickleness of Greek fortunes.

British troops made a Commando raid on Castelorizo early in the Second World War, and in its later stages occupied the island. Their legacy to it was to burn down half the town. We walked back to the quayside through its ruins, tidily stacked by the Greeks in heaps of stone, with broad paved lanes and steps between them. But even the half that remained would soon be too large for the dwindling population. Castelorizo is dying—but, in the Greek fashion, dying on its feet. The people who gathered around us, in the waterfront café, had little to do, and less to eat than the Turks in the cafés of Andifli opposite. But they listened eagerly, talked alertly. The café was bare, but there was *ouzo* to drink, with a *mezze* composed of a few fragments of goat's meat, a sliver of tripe, and some bony little fish, called irreverently 'nuns', from their evident pregnancy. The Mayor explained this to us, a pale alive old man with few teeth in his head but a philosophic intelligence, and a sense of the eternal history of the Wandering Greek. In the heyday of the island he was a prosperous merchant, dealing in timber, enjoying a fortune equal to £100,000 in sterling. The decline of Castelorizo began, he said, when the Italians, during the Tripolitanian War, destroyed its ships. Emigration then started—mainly to Australia. It increased between the wars, and now amounted almost to an evacuation. Those who stayed could get little from the stony waterless soil, and lived largely on remittances from Athens and America. If the fishermen poached the Turkish waters, who could blame them? The Turks did not trouble, or did not know how to fish them.

With the Mayor, speaking French, was a holiday visitor, who had come on the irregular supply boat from Athens for a fortnight's fishing. What Turkish visitor from Istanbul would do likewise? The single Adonis of the town, his dark eyes flashing, his locks well oiled, his skin tanned dark by the sun, swaggered carelessly past us, showing off before a huddle of women who squatted discreetly apart. Affecting indifference, they turned instead to follow us with their eyes as we strolled back to the *Elfin*. A local mechanic had been repairing her engines. The Consul-General tried to pay him, but he waved the money aside. He would prefer a note to the British Consul-General in Rhodes, who could help him to get to Australia. Amid farewell greetings we sailed away from the island, across the channel to that other slower, more silent world of the Anatolian mainland. It seemed a wasteful miscarriage of history that had deprived each of the benefit of the other's good qualities.

* * *

Next morning we anchored for breakfast and a bathe in the lee of a great arch, carved by nature out of the pliant limestone cliff. Wide in span as the arch of Ctesiphon, it led into a cave like the vault of a cathedral, where the cradled sea rocked gently against walls of polished stone. Before it the cliffs in their strata swirled this way and that, now with an upward, now with a downward sweep, creations of the sea and the rain which mould them, the sun and the wind which colour them. Diving into the limpid turquoise water, I saw how the sea forever builds the rock, coating the surface with its own organic matter, glowing algae of yellow and violet. Above water I saw how it petrifies, drying and hardening to a duller yellow, sprayed with black; how the rock grows smoother and its colours warmer in the wind and the sunlight, yellow bleaching to white, then weathering to gold, black weathering to grey through a gradation of bolder mineral patterns; how as it rises new organic matter, not of the sea but of the earth, starts in its turn to build, coating the surface with new patterns, while a new moisture from the skies seeps down into the stone, crumbling and rending it apart, into new, cataclysmic forms. Thus the cliff towered before us, a monument to nature's capacity to create art, now abstract, now Romantic, on a superhuman scale.

Beyond the headland, off the beach where Patara lies, a boisterous sea was running. Rather than land there, we scaled the cliff to walk to the ruined Lycian city, bidding the captain come for us in two hours' time. A long white sand-bank, with a foreshore of polished shingle, lay before us, promising a smooth and easy walk. As at Demre, the sea had built it up through the centuries to isolate the city, the port where St. Paul had landed. Among the dunes, in the distance, we noticed a small police post. Waving to the gendarmes, we strode ahead, cooling our feet in the waves which lapped the burning sands. Fellows, when he came here, prophesied that with the advance of the sand, the city, one of the six in the Lycian League, would 'soon be entirely buried, and left for future ages to disinter'. He was over-pessimistic. Climbing up through the dunes to the high ground, we looked down over its widespread Roman ruins, stretching away over stubble fields towards a triple triumphal gateway. Here was a sweep of fertile land, part of the valley of the Xanthus,[1] the sacred river of Lycia—as of Troy, where its warriors fought so staunchly—and commanded at its head by the range of Mount Cragus, now called by the Turks, like so many high peaks, Ak Dağ. Patara was a place renowned in Roman times for its gilded sandals. But above all it was a centre, second only to Delphi, of the cult of Apollo: the Lycian Apollo, transported from Crete by its earliest colonists. Leto, according to Lycian legend, was brought here by the wolves, to give birth to Apollo and Artemis, whom she then bathed in the Xanthus.

On the headland where we stood was a curious pit, deep as a well, with downward steps and a pillar arising from its centre. Beaufort thinks that this may have been the seat of the oracle, and that a statue once stood on the pillar. More probably it was some kind of lighthouse where a beacon was lit for the guidance of ships entering the harbour. Today the sea is far away from it, beyond the dunes, while the harbour, already too small in classical times to contain the joint fleet of the

[1] Now the Koca.

Romans, Rhodians and their Greek allies,[1] is now no more than a land-locked marsh. On the edge of it is a large stone building, like that at Demre, built in the time of the Emperor Hadrian for the storage of grain. After exploring the remains of the Roman theatre, carved out of the hillside and partially buried by sand-drifts, we determined to visit it.

But before us there suddenly appeared three gendarmes, from the police post, down by the beach. What, they asked, was our business? We had come, the Consul-General explained, to visit the antiquities of Patara. Where had we come from? From our boat, the *Elfin*, which was sheltering out of sight, beyond the headland, and would presently come to fetch us. Who were we, and where were our passports? We were the English *Baş Konsolos* and an exalted English senator. Our passports were on the boat. Since we had been bathing, and were only wearing shorts, as they could see, we had not brought them with us.

At once a dispute broke out between the gendarmes: two who did not believe us against one who did. The Consul-General called impatiently for silence, and asked which of the three was in command. It was the one who believed us: a nice-looking youth, carrying a Sten gun, who said that his name was Ali. Very well, said the Consul-General, let Ali accompany us to Hadrian's granary and back, by which time our boat should have arrived. The youth agreed. The more aggressive of the others, a surly long-faced individual with a loping gait, wearing patches on his knees and a green plastic belt, made as if to protest. But the Consul-General silenced him, with a flow of withering comments on his inferior rank. Unarmed, he hung back sulkily with his companion, an unshaven boy with a revolver, while we walked ahead with Ali.

We had not gone far when there was a disturbance behind us. We turned to see that a fourth gendarme had joined the party. He had a rifle, which the loper had snatched from him, and was now brandishing in our direction. The newcomer called on us to return. Our escort indignantly refused. This was mutiny. The loper loaded his rifle, and levelled it towards the three of us, about to fire. It was time to go quietly. As we walked back across the stubble fields, under arrest, the Consul-General was far from quiet. Who, he asked once more, was in

[1] Livy, quoted by W. M. Leake, *Journal of a Tour in Asia Minor*. London: 1824.

command? This time it was the newcomer, a hook-nosed, hirsute individual, in a tunic and a torn blue shirt, who proclaimed himself a corporal. Where then, the Consul-General demanded, were his badges of rank? Having none, he was silent; but the loper muttered triumphantly: '*Baş Konsolos*, indeed! *We'll* soon see who you are. . . . Boat indeed! A fine story. You know well there's no boat.' They did not know, it seemed, what a Consul was. '*Baş Konsolos*' made them only more suspicious, and when the Consul-General tried '*General Konsolos*,' they replied: 'We obey no generals but those of the Turkish Army.'

Back at the police post, we found a row of six beds with hard mattresses of sackcloth, beneath an awning of brushwood. Here, while the corporal tried at the top of his voice to telephone, we relaxed, surveying the white sands and the sunlit seascape. As we did so the *Elfin* sailed into the picture, punctual to the hour. The Consul-General pointed to her in triumph. The corporal came out, looking sheepish, now wearing his stripes. We processed down to the beach, where our captors, fearful of a wetting, removed their trousers and stood in their long white pants. The sea was still rough, and the dinghy could not easily reach the shore. Impatiently the Consul-General removed his shorts and strode towards it into the waves, a formidable figure in only a Panama hat, with a shirt tucked up above a fine white behind. With sudden misgiving the corporal tore off his pants, revealing hairs curling upwards from sinewy legs with the luxuriance of water-weeds, and prepared to follow him. But his dignity got the better of him, and, rather than flaunt his nakedness before our crew, he remained, content to hold me as a hostage.

The Consul-General waded ashore again, the passports wrapped in his shirt, together with the ship's papers and a letter from a high Turkish authority, vouching for his status to all whom it might concern. The gendarmes in their pants, and the corporal, still without his, pored over the documents in a huddle, while one, who could read, spelt them out laboriously, word by word, like a lesson in school. Assuming that we had arrived from some foreign land, they were nonplussed to find that the *Elfin* was manned by Turks and that her papers were Turkish. The corporal returned to the police post to fetch a copybook, in which, squatting on the sand, he began with a stub of pencil to write down our names and an account of the incident. But the Consul-General hustled him on board, where he could sit at a table. The youth Ali accompanied him, standing guard over us in his pants, with a rifle. But after a moment, with the boat's gentle rocking, both were obliged, looking pale, to retire. The revenge was sweet.

The corporal, now chastened, expressed the hope to the crew that the Consul-General would not put in an unfavourable report.

'We must carry out orders,' he explained. 'We are told to stop any man or beast who passes this way.'

But the Consul-General, I suspected, was already coining indignant phrases in his head. They were curious orders, in a country which has forsworn xenophobia.

* * *

Beyond the mouth of the Xanthus the lofty range of the Seven Capes piled itself up before us, sheer from the sea. Once I had climbed its topmost peak, now Baba Dağ, with my botanist friend Peter Davis, riding up through a forest of cedars to reach an Alpine *yayla* flowing with the blessed sour milk of the mountains; then after a night in the open, walking the last steep lap beyond the tree-line, to the bare and sunlit peak. Scrambling down the opposite slope towards the Xanthus,[1] we had found, with some difficulty, the overgrown city of Pinara, another of the Lycian six, where Pandarus was worshipped and may even have lived.[2] A deep ravine, pitted with Lycian tombs, led through to the ruins which lay in a cleft like a punch-bowl, beneath the mountains. Struggling through a tangle of scrub, we had found the stones of an elegant theatre, small as an Odeon, described by Fellows, who must have seen more of it, 'as the most highly and expensively finished that I have seen'.

Now, as the evening light fell on the *Elfin's* deck, the Seven Capes became an intangible pink silhouette, beneath golden wraiths of cloud. As we chugged up the long gulf of Fethiye, the scent of pines drifted out to us from the darkening land, to sweeten the tang of the sea, while the moon flung a glittering flarepath across it, as though to pilot us into the harbour. Here a cruder, more garish light greeted us. Since my last visit a democratic régime had blessed Fethiye with the benefits of electricity, which now blazed down on the waterfront in all its

[1] Dr. P. H. Davis, in *The Journal of the Royal Horticultural Society*, Vol. LXXIV, Parts 3 and 4, describes an *Echinops* which we found on our scramble. 'The heads can be nearly six inches across—incredible spheres of pale jade green. As these eccentric baubles are carried on stems of no more than eighteen inches, it was a great disappointment that the seed of this wonderful species could not be obtained.'

[2] Strabo. *Geography*. Book XIV.

naked fluorescence. The haphazard coffee-garden, beneath the three eucalyptus trees, had been enclosed by a nice concrete wall, with a concrete pavement. Moreover the people of Fethiye had learnt also the pleasures of advertisement. Stretching across the entire first floor of the Ak Deniz coffee-shop was a poster of monstrous size, advertising a brand of shirts and pyjamas. Next morning an aeroplane circled the town, dropping cakes of soap by parachute. A small boy was driving a tractor along the quay, and the shops reflected the new era of peasant prosperity, displaying radios, electric irons and refrigerators, among their familiar cheapjack merchandise. The market for these, in the villages of modern Turkey, is unaffected by their lack of electric power. A refrigerator stands proudly in the living-room, a symbol of wealth, often unused, but sometimes fitted with lock and key, and used as a safe for the storage of gold and banknotes.

For all that, Fethiye was still a flyblown little place, lying in a kind of luminous stagnation in the shelter of its waveless gulf. An almost tropical paralysis, alien to the Mediterranean, gripped its inhabitants, who sat through the evening sipping their coffee in sultry silence, before the two rival coffee-shops with rival loudspeakers: the Ak Deniz, furnished with kitchen chairs, for the ordinary citizens; the Şehir Külübü, or City Club, where superior gentlemen lounged in basket chairs, beneath a Doric portico, with an air of some self-importance. A livelier individual greeted us, Hasan the fisherman, who had taken me across to Rhodes, a night's journey in his motor-boat, two years before, and who was now hoping for a job from the Consul-General on board the *Elfin*. With a raucous laugh he recalled how, on the voyage, he had pummelled me, lying flat on my face amidships, in an attempt to ease an attack of lumbago. It is an ailment common in these parts, where chill breezes strike suddenly on perspiring limbs—hence, perhaps, the Turkish cummerbund. Hasan certainly wore his as a precaution against it, wound in thick woollen layers around his loins, and like most Turks he had a rudimentary experience of massage. Now he insisted on taking us across the harbour for a ride in his new boat, which he had painted up in bright colours and embellished with his photograph and other decorative features. Then he stood us bottles of lemonade, in a bleak new café which had been opened at the foot of a projected new jetty. From nearby there were sounds of hubbub, of cries and shots, which rang through the town and momentarily drew our attention. But they came only from the local open-air cinema.

Hasan, like most of the population of Fethiye, had not much to say for the Greeks. His indeed was the only boat to do the journey from here to Rhodes, which had little other contact with the Turkish mainland. A Greek boat seldom came into Fethiye. Lately a Greek Customs launch, with a party of *Air France* officials searching for the wreckage of a plane which had crashed in the straits, had done so. The captain found that he had no Turkish flag to hoist in Turkish waters. The harbour-master hurriedly produced one, and passed it to the captain, who tossed it to a Greek sailor. The wind caught the flag, but the sailor, with some presence of mind, put his foot on it, and thus saved it from blowing overboard. Seeing the Turkish flag thus trampled underfoot by a Greek, the people of Fethiye became enraged, and made an ugly disturbance, which had to be quelled by the police. They arrested the captain and his crew, who were held for a day until orders arrived from a higher authority to release them. The *Kaymakam*, held responsible, was transferred elsewhere, and now all was quiet. The customary curtain between Turkey and the islands had fallen once more.

When Fellows visited it, Fethiye, otherwise Makri, was inhabited principally by Greeks, trading in timber and its by-products. That was before the days of chrome, now its principal export. It was an unhealthy malarial spot, and when Sir Sidney Smith put in here in the *Tigre*, he had a hundred of his crew on the sick-list within a week. Dr. Clarke, who records this in his *Travels*, ascribes the malaria to the 'mephitic exhalations of carburetted hydrogen', arising from improperly drained land. The author himself 'soon became a striking example of the powerful influence of such air, not only in the fever which then attacked him, but in a temporary privation of the use of his limbs, which continued until he put to sea again'.[1] The land is now well enough drained, and malaria is no longer a scourge.

As the classical Telmessus, the town was renowned for its supremacy in the art of divination. It had a college of soothsayers, who were consulted on many historic occasions. Croesus, King of Lydia, sent a delegation here at the outset of his campaign against the Persians.[2] Alexander, coming here after the siege of Halicarnassus, consulted the oracles as to the secret of his future.[3] Nothing remains today of the theatre of Telmessus, described by Texier and the other travellers of

[1] E. D. Clarke. *Travels in Europe, Asia and Africa*. Vol. III. London: 1817.

[2] Herodotus. *History*. Book I.

[3] Arrian. *Anabasis*. Book I.

his period. But the city survives in a number of tombs, cut out of the cliff which surmounts the harbour. Three of them have imposing classical façades, with Ionic columns, lofty entablatures and studded doorways of stone, which have almost weathered into iron. Had some English nobleman of the eighteenth century seen these elegant tombs, as he saw the temples of the Greeks and Romans, nearer home, they might well have been reproduced as a decorative fancy, carved from a cliff in some park in the Dukeries. Their Grecian style contrasts with the more native Lycian style of other tombs around them. Texier, commenting on this, dates them from the time of Alexander. He must have examined them thoroughly, since his signature, still as clear as new, can be seen carved on one of them, twenty feet from the ground.

CHAPTER 6

CARIA (I)

The Gulf of Marmaris—Sponge Fishers of Bozburun—A Statue of Demeter—Cnidus and its Treasures—In a Classical Harbour—The Lights of Cos

'THE APPEARANCE of all the south of Asia Minor, from the sea,' wrote Dr. Clarke, 'is fearfully grand, and perhaps no part of it possesses more eminently those sources of the sublime which Burke has instructed us to find in vastness and terror, than the entrance to the gulph into which we were now sailing.' Sailing out of it, beneath the midday sun, it was easy to agree with him. Here behind us was the grand finale of the Taurus, its giant grey limbs subsiding smoothly into the plain, while its familiar cluster of satellite hills bowed for the last time before it. The free poetic line of the range now ebbed away into the lower, more prosaic, formal slopes of the Dorian promontory, thrusting peninsulas and islands westwards into the world of the Aegean. This was Caria, which the Dorians had colonized, finding a people who, in the view of Herodotus, were not indigenous to Asia Minor, but had come from the islands of the Aegean.[1] They were a race of warriors and pirates, whom King Minos of Crete had expelled to the mainland of Asia Minor, proceeding nevertheless to make use of their naval skill in the expansion of his empire. The Dorians in their turn, establishing settlements on the coast, drove them eastwards and inland, until they were finally subdued by the Lydians.[2]

Following our usual habit, we anchored for the afternoon in the shade of a cliff. Before a *raki* and luncheon I dived down in goggles into the ultra-violet submarine world, tracing the rock to its foundations amid rounded boulders and pits like a giant's footprints. Here was

[1] *History*. Book I.

[2] J. A. Cramer. *Geographical and Historical Description of Asia Minor*. Oxford: 1832.

a life of weeds with waving tresses, of roving fish with a rainbow gleam, of colonies of sea-urchins, purple and treacherous, cushioning the smooth white rocks. Towards evening we sailed through the narrow channel which leads into the Gulf of Marmaris. The gulf is in effect a deep, secluded lagoon, a favourite anchorage of the British Mediterranean Fleet since the time of Sir Sidney Smith. Unfortunately, on a recent visit to hold their annual regatta, they are reputed to have set fire to part of the surrounding hillsides, and have since tactfully held it elsewhere.

The small port of Marmaris lay compactly piled at the head of the gulf, around the towers and walls of a mediaeval castle. Greek in aspect, its whitewashed houses, with red-tiled roofs and tall white chimneys, sea-blue shutters and vine-covered balconies, stood on firm foundations of mellowed golden stone. Along the harbour the insubstantial plastered houses were painted in a graceful confusion of clashing blues and chocolates and greys, with whitewashed windows and shutters in contrasting colours. Here and there even corrugated iron had been turned to decorative account. Used in long vertical panels, painted green, it gave an elegant fluted look to a façade. The streets were still cobbled, but there were sinister signs of approaching prosperity. Pylons, not lamp-posts, awaited the arrival of the electric light, while on the main square Atatürk was up to his neck in gravel, part of the litter which arose from the construction of a pier. In a Spor Külübü the youth of Marmaris played ping-pong; in a smoky coffee-house opposite their elders played cards. From here we were removed by the local doctor, who took us away to a bleaker, more refined establishment, further down the quay. He was a native of Thrace, a far cry from Lycia. His hair was wavy and fair, and he was proud of his costume —a pyjama jacket, Glenurquhart tweed trousers and grey suède shoes.

The Doctor spoke confident English. The Burgomaster, he regretted, had gone off to inspect a new highway. He himself, as an Anglophil, was delighted to entertain us in his place.

'Like the English,' he said, 'I am a sportsmanship.'

We sat with him for an hour in the heat of the night, too listless to return to the *Elfin*. As other citizens joined us the Doctor greeted them.

'In Turkey,' he explained, 'we have an old-fashioned custom. When other ones come to his table we say to him, "Hullo! Hullo! Hullo!" '

* * *

We were now on a Greek, no longer a Roman coast—the Rhodian Perea, where cliffs swirled up from the sea-bed, rugged, white and gold. Next afternoon we sailed beneath the walls of Loryma, a long, grey fortress, crowning a cape which is the nearest point to Rhodes. It is a Hellenistic city, which now stands alone, remote from any modern habitation. Its ample blocks of stone, well-faced and well-jointed, its broad low symmetrical bastions give it a streamlined dignity, such as the Romans, cruder and more ponderous, seldom achieved.

As the coast-line ebbs away westwards, its harbours follow one another in a similar pattern but on a diminishing scale. Marmaris, within its secluded gulf, is a smaller version of Fethiye; Bozburun, similarly sheltered, is a smaller version of Marmaris, so small indeed that it has a mere dozen houses, and a single café with a brushwood roof. Protocol was nevertheless strictly observed on our arrival. A round-headed captain of gendarmerie shepherded us away from the café to the office of a lean Chief of Police, who gave us our first cup of coffee, seated on upright chairs outside. We were then summoned to the office of the *Nahiye Müdür* who gave us our second cup, seated in leather chairs inside. Windows shut out the evening air, and an acetylene lamp so warmed the room that as the Consul-General and *Müdür* discussed local affairs I grew impatient and restive, seeking air. There was in fact little to talk about but the sponge-fishing industry, on which Bozburun survived. Here, around the Gulf of Symi, are some hundred families of Turkish sponge-fishers, and we were to pass their boats at anchor, festooned with drying sponges, while the fishermen dived, down to a depth of eighty metres. In season they do well from the sponges, making a profit of thirty-three and a third per cent.—perhaps £1 per day. The Greek sponge-fishers, on the island of Symi opposite, like to drink away their money on brandy and *ouzo* and their wives will wait by the hour on the quay to take it off them, before they can do so. But the Turkish sponge-fishers spend the money on gold which they hang around the necks of their wives. In the previous year they had made a remarkable catch in these waters, a bronze statue of the goddess Demeter, of the fourth century B.C. It must have been shipwrecked on its way to or from one of the Greek cities of the coast.

Soon after dawn next morning we sailed close by the rocks of Symi, where nature is barren but man is prolific. Against the dead brown hillside a live white town clambered vigorously upwards, the cubes of its houses and the domes of its churches covering the nakedness of the land, its windows gazing forever like eyes out to sea and across to the empty Turkish mainland. Two strings of Greek fishing-boats, their lamps now extinguished, were bringing in the night's catch, much as the Dorians must have done here before Homer was born. Symi was the home of Nireus, reputed, during the Trojan War, to be the handsomest Greek after Achilles.

We were now approaching the sacred capital of the later Dorian League, the city of Cnidus, which graced the tail of the Dorian promontory. This is the south-westerly tip of the Turkish continent. Known to the ancients as Doris or Triopion, to modern Greeks and Italians as Cape Crio, to the Turks as the Deveboyun, and to mariners, battling around it throughout the centuries, as a treacherous headland with a merciful harbour in the lee of it, Cnidus was founded as a colony by a Lacedaemonian, Triopas, and flourished from the seventh century B.C. onwards. It was dedicated to Apollo, his temple crowned the headland, and the Triopian games were held there in his honour by the cities of the League, a hexapolis reduced to a pentapolis by the misbehaviour and expulsion of Halicarnassus.

Here the familiar white limestone gives place to a harder, redder rock, like porphyry, boldly stratified with marble in a dramatic sequence of patterns, as though challenging man to build on it. And indeed he had done so. One of these rocks a mile or so east of the Triopion was the massive 'pedestal' of the statue of a lion, discovered in 1857 by Newton, 'the mad English Consul who was digging holes in the ground at Cape Crio'.[1] Hewn in the fourth century B.C. from a single block of Pentelic marble, he had once surmounted a Doric tomb, but had fallen on his side, breaking his jaw and burying his nose in the ground, and had been thought by the Turks to be no more than a rock. When lifted, the lion 'mounted slowly and majestically into the air, as if a Michael Angelo had said to him "Arise!" . . . When our eyes met for the first time his calm, majestic gaze, it seemed as if we had suddenly roused him from his sleep of ages'. The removal to a warship and hence to the British Museum of this 'colossal prize', eleven tons in weight, was a formidable task. It took a hundred Turks three days to get the statue to a boat, and the corporal, who accompanied the Consul, remarked drily that they were 'very lucky not to have had

[1] C. T. Newton. *Travels and Discoveries in the Levant*. London: 1865.

a heavy butcher's bill to settle'. He suggests that the monument may have been a war memorial, built after the great naval battle off Cnidus, when the Athenians defeated the Spartans.[1]

'The lion', writes Newton, 'seemed made for the scenery, the scenery for the lion.' Indeed the Triopion itself, a slice of rock curving sharply upwards, then breaking off abruptly, as though leaving the continent of Asia unfinished, looks from the seaward side like some corrugated dome-headed lion, mounting guard with its paws in the waves. Here only a few broken marbles, scattered around the scrub, suggest where a temple may once have stood. A modern light-house now stands in its place. But the slope, where shrubs crouch, splayed against the rock by the fierce prevailing winds, remains still firmly terraced by the smooth, consummate masonry of the Greeks. Here are monumental stones, so faced and chiselled that they fit together without mortar, making walls indestructible.

The Triopion is almost an island. On the mainland it is complemented by a broader, more gradual sweep of land, curving up to a ridge where the classical citadel stands, and here the rest of the city of Cnidus was built. Only a narrow isthmus, described by Strabo as a mole,[2] links the two, giving protection to two snug harbours. We came alongside in the larger, more easterly anchorage, Strabo's 'naval station for twenty vessels', disembarking on a quay which Greeks must have built during the Alexandrine age. Partly carved out of the rock, it is reinforced and paved with regular slabs of stone, broken by stairways and bounded by walls where the rock subsides. From either bank they have thrown out a breakwater, made of great stone blocks, down to a hundred feet deep, to protect the harbour mouth, while a long sea-wall continues the line of the quays, giving an urban appearance to the port. The smaller harbour, 'fit for receiving triremes', faces towards the West. Here openings have been made in the rock to enable the boats to be dragged on shore. The narrow entrance, once closed by a chain, is defended by a broad round tower, rising up from the sea-wall, austerely functional, built of smooth clean masonry and so weathered as to look like new. Beneath it a canal of green water, cleaving the blue, shows where the channel has been widened artificially.

On the isthmus, between the two harbours, below the site where the

[1] It was removed to the cellars of the British Museum on the outbreak of the Second World War, and has not yet been moved back into the galleries.

[2] *Geography*. Book XIV.

Temple of Dionysus stood, we found a post of gendarmes, a mixed lot of youths who betrayed in their features the polyglot nature of the Turks. Already familiar with the *Elfin*, they greeted us warmly. The Consul-General's account of our arrest at Patara diverted them, and they laughed scornfully at the folly of their colleagues. But suspicion of the foreigner was still deeply inbred in them. For whom, we asked them, were they keeping watch so studiously?

'For enemies,' they said, with a sweep of the arm towards the spectral forms of the Dodecanese Islands, opposite. 'For the Italians . . . for the Greeks . . .'

'But the Italians are there no more, and the Greeks are your allies.'

They smiled incredulously and continued their watch.

Inland, girdles of classical wall ring the hillside, rising tier above tier up to a protective ridge, whose rocky defences are reinforced by a stout chain of battlements. At first sight little remains of the city but these walls, once the foundations of public buildings and baths and temples, now mere terraces for the fields of Turkish peasants—but terraces built on a noble and enduring scale, such as peasants seldom achieve. Much of the stone has been quarried since the Dilettanti Society excavated the site in the early nineteenth century: Mohammed Aly, in the eighteen-thirties, removed several shiploads of its marble to build his palace in Cairo. But the eye of the antiquarian sees further traces. Here a larger wall emerges, above a fallen colonnade, there a ring of stones form an amphitheatre, here a large space of ground has been levelled for an *agora*, there, beneath the cliff of the Acropolis, a rock projects, smoothed as the base of the Temple of Demeter, for which the sponge-fishers' statue may well have been destined. Among its ruins Newton found curious votive objects, including, to his embarrassment, marble effigies of a pig, the unclean animal of the Moslems. But his Turkish workmen referred to them as bears, 'a pious and convenient euphemism in which I was quite ready to acquiesce'.

In Newton's time a powerful *Agha* ruled this peninsula, a man with four harems, who was said to be the father of half the children in his village. He was a shrewd man of business, 'who ought to have been a Scotchman', and carried on an active trade with Smyrna. He was also a keen historian, speaking familiarly of Iskander (Alexander), Plato, Aristotle, and Bokrat (Hippocrates), 'all of whom he conceived to have lived in the same generation, and to have been on very intimate terms'. Today there was no such company at Cnidus, indeed apart from the gendarmes no sign of human life. In classical times the place was famous for its wine, the best in Asiatic Greece, for its vinegar, second only to that of Egypt, for its reed pens, better than those of Egypt, for its white poplars, producing a scented ointment, and for its onions, renowned for their mildness.[1] But today, amid a tangle of wild thyme and statice, nothing grew but a sparse crop of wheat.

Out to sea, crouching low on the water, lay three vigilant rocks, lion-cubs as it were, with manes of stone, thrown out by the cliff to protect it. Beyond them the archipelago danced away towards Greece, like a menagerie of mythical beasts. Islands posed for our pleasure, relieving the eye whichever way we looked. To the west Cos reared its forceful head, above the hard volcanic pate of Nisiros, then stretched its length upon the sea like a long-tailed dragon, the waves breaking white over its haunches. Cos, as a religious centre, was the unsuccessful rival of Cnidus. When Praxiteles came to Caria, to inspect the work on the Mausoleum at Halicarnassus, both cities commissioned a statue from him. Cnidus ordered a nude Aphrodite, Cos preferred her draped. Praxiteles duly produced two masterpieces, which became the pride of their respective cities. But whereas the nude Aphrodite brought Cnidus a thriving trade in pilgrims, the draped goddess attracted few visitors, and Cos, thus falling into debt, could not raise the full money to pay for her.[2]

Meanwhile for centuries people came from all parts of the world to see the beauties of the Aphrodite, later the Venus of Cnidus, whose cult must have superseded that of Apollo. The King of Bithynia offered to remit to the Cnidians the whole of their public debt, which was considerable, if they would cede him the statue: but they refused to give it up.[3] Lucian, describing the temple, which 'abounds with productive trees, extending their luxuriant foliage to the sky, and canopying the air around', and with 'pleasant seats for convivial meetings' in its deeper shades, grows lyrical over the statue with the 'half suppressed smile' on her mouth. 'The rigid and repulsive marble', he writes, 'perfectly represents the delicate formation of every limb . . . the harmony of the back, the wonderful fitting of the flesh to the bones, without too great plumpness, and the exquisite proportion of thigh and

[1] Quoted from Pliny and other sources by the Dilettanti Society. *Ionian Antiquities*. London: 1769.

[2] Saturnino Ximinez. *Asia Minor in Ruins*. London: 1925.

[3] Pliny, quoted in *Ionian Antiquities*.

leg, ending in a straight line to the foot'. His friend Charicles, 'as if bereft of his senses, cried aloud: "Happy amongst the gods he that was enchained for thee"; and springing forward with neck outstretched as far as possible, he repeatedly kissed the statue'.[1] The statue remained at Cnidus until the fifth century A.D. when, together with other classical loot from these parts, it was removed to Constantinople by the Emperor Theodosius. There it was destroyed in a fire, which also consumed the imperial library of a hundred and twenty thousand books, including a unique copy of the *Iliad* and the *Odyssey*, written in letters of gold on the intestines of a serpent a hundred and twenty feet in length.[2]

* * *

After a final bathe in the naval harbour, we sailed out of Cnidus into the velvet night beneath a voluminous skull-cap of stars. The two lighthouses winked across at each other, with punctilious monotony: two flashes from Cnidus, one flash from Cos, their beams sweeping low over the sea. Five brighter stars, strung out in a line, shone on the water itself—the acetylene lamps of the Greek fishermen, who had just put out from the harbour. We coasted close to the shore of the island, so close indeed that we almost ran aground, in rapidly shallowing water. Disengaging ourselves, to my faint regret, we saw ahead of us a broader bar of light, the electric street-lamps of Halicarnassus. Punctually at midnight they went out. The town was asleep when we glided into the harbour and anchored beneath the walls of the massive mediaeval castle.

[1] Lucian. *Amores.*

[2] Quoted in *Ionian Antiquities. op. cit.*

CHAPTER 7

CARIA (2)

Halicarnassus—Macabre Quest of a Sponge Fisher—Early Bedtime in Bodrum—Hermaphroditus—The Castle of the Knights—Jacks-of-All-Trades—The End of the Mausoleum

IT WAS THREE YEARS EARLIER, in autumn weather, that I had first visited Halicarnassus, reaching it by bus from inland and spending a night on the way at Milas. This was Mylasa, a city built beneath a marble quarry, hence, according to Strabo, 'beautifully adorned with porticoes and temples'.[1] Nothing remains of them today but an elegant Roman mausoleum, such as any English nobleman would be proud to have in his park. Inspired perhaps by the Mausoleum of Halicarnassus, but on a miniature scale, it consists of a square, Corinthian colonnade with a pyramidal roof and a hole in its floor, surmounting a dark sepulchral chamber. There are differing theories as to the purpose of the hole. Pococke declared that he who stood beneath it received on his garments the sanctifying blood of the sacrifice, and wore them thereafter until they fell to pieces.[2] The Turks told Fellows that the building was a treasury, and that gold was poured through the hole into the strong-room below. More convincingly, according to Chandler, the ashes of the deceased lay in the lower chamber, while his relatives and friends gathered annually in the upper, to pour libations of milk, honey or wine through the hole, thus gratifying his spirit.[3]

Next day, as we jolted westwards, a grey sou'-wester drove in from the sea, to envelop the landscape in a soft persistent rain. The smell of it was as familiar as the smell of Cornwall or the Mull of Kintyre. Growing fiercer, the rain turned the earth road, with its potholes, into a swirling river of apricot slush. When we arrived in Bodrum (as

[1] *Geography*. Book XIV.

[2] Richard Pococke. *Description of the East*. London: 1745.

[3] R. Chandler. *Travels in Asia Minor*. London: 1817.

Halicarnassus now is) it had become a downpour: a downpour, moreover, which continued, with mounting ferocity, throughout the rest of the day and the night. A dark, lugubrious individual, with a bald head tapering to a point, had attached himself to me in the bus as a guide: Halil Sungerci by name—Halil the Sponge Fisher. He sat down beside me as I ate my lunch in a *lokanta*, drinking a bottle of beer. Out of politeness I offered him a drink. He ordered and drank half a bottle of *raki*. Escaping, I huddled beneath blankets in one of the large draughty rooms of a rickety caravanserai. Later I tried to visit the castle. The guide, sensibly enough on such a torrential afternoon, was not there. The Sponge Fisher, swaying a little and still smelling of the *raki*, went off and returned with him in a quarter of an hour, saying he had had to take a taxi to the other end of the town, and it would cost me a pound. Angrily, taking in the whole town at a glance, I paid him five shillings. The castle looked out on to a sick green sea, enveloped in blankets of cloud. I padded around it in the rain, then returned to my bedroom.

The Sponge Fisher followed me there, lurching around the room and in a thick voice trying to tell me some story. Laboriously, in Turkish, he reiterated phrase after phrase. Finally I understood him. While diving for sponges he had found in deep water the wrecks of several aircraft, which had crashed here during the war, shot down perhaps over Rhodes. Three of them were British, and in the cabin of one there were still three bodies—bodies of R.A.F. airmen, in good condition. He knew exactly where they lay. What would I pay him to bring them up? It was a macabre proposition, up here in this ramshackle room, with the rain pounding on the roof and seeping through the windows and the Sponge Fisher swaying over the bed like some elongated spectre, in the light of the guttering lamp. I promised to speak of the matter to the Air Attaché or the Consul-General. The Sponge Fisher, dreaming of an immediate fortune, was disconsolate. He asked if I would like to buy some valuable old coins, and brought out a handful of modern ones, with a button or two thrown in. Rejecting them, but consoling him with another five shillings, I ushered him out into the rain.[1]

Towards seven o'clock in the evening I went out in search of a meal.

[1] Nothing came of the project to raise the bodies, but I was glad to hear that the Consul-General, visiting Bodrum later, had helped to get the Sponge Fisher a job in Izmir.

But no restaurant was open. They closed, I learnt, at 6.30 p.m. I dined off a biscuit and a bowl of *yoğurt* in a milk-shop, which flaunted a few small sponges, wrapped in cellophane and mounted on coral, in the window. Enlivening its walls were an Arabic text, an old photograph of Atatürk, and the Technicolor effigy of an American cover-girl, advertising a brand of radio. The Sponge Fisher, to my relief, had vanished, but I was joined by a new companion, a youth with swimming brown eyes, closely-curled black hair, and features of a sallower, finer clay. He was, he said in English, an Istanbuli, condemned to lodge here with his aunt to finish his secondary schooling. He spoke of Bodrum and its people with the amused contempt of a young sophisticate, the man of culture marooned among barbarians.

'Is it always so dead in the evenings?' I asked.

'Always,' he said. 'There's no cinema, nothing.'

'Why not?'

'The people won't spend their money. They stay at home in the evenings.'

'And what do they do at home?'

'They go to bed.' He gave a ripple of laughter, and added: 'In the dark. The town put up a generator. But the people won't pay to put in the electric light. They grow fruit, but they will not eat it. They send it all to Istanbul for money.'

'And where does their money go to?'

'Where do you think?' he replied, with a scornful twinkle. 'They spend it on necklaces of gold coins, for their wives.'

'They have plenty of it?'

'Not so much. They can't sell their sponges. The Greeks are more clever. They have all the trade.'

I stood him a glass of milk. The waiter tried to turn on the radio, but he protested: 'There's nothing but Turkish music.' Sugaring the milk, he went on: 'They do not even come to school. We have only twenty new pupils in two years. Instead, when they are sixteen they start to drink *raki*.'

'You play games at school?'

'Yes, volley-ball, basket, swimming.'

'Not football?'

'Not football. If I play football perhaps I break my leg. Then the girls, they will not like me.' He laughed with a roguish air. 'You think I speak well English?'

'Very well.'

'Every day I write my diary, in English. You like to see it?'

It was a diary such as Gide might have commended, with translations of romantic Turkish poems and revelations of love for a comrade: 'I wait for him one hour. He do not come. I despair. I do not sleep. I decide never I see him again.'

He interrupted me as I read: 'You play cheese?'

'You mean chess?'

'It is chess? I am so sorry. I will remember.'

'No, not tonight.'

It was only eight o'clock, but the waiter was yawning, the street was dead, the milk-shop was chilly. Halicarnassus was no place for chess. It was time to creep once more beneath those blankets, hoping for sleep in the monotony of the rain hammering down on the roof.

Next morning it had stopped, clearing the sky for the sun, leaving the sea an unhealthy livid yellow. In the milk-shop I had an excellent breakfast of hot sweet milk, fresh bread, quince jam and butter. The youth was there, drinking his milk, writing laboriously in his diary. He took me to see the house where he lived with his aunt, a large, square house, plastered yellow, on the eastern bay. Here the houses give on to the sea, for this was once the quarter of the Greeks. On the western bay, which was the Turkish quarter, they stand back from it, behind high harem walls. My companion wanted to show me the rest of the town. Perhaps ungraciously I shook him off. I wanted a long swift walk to the point of the headland, which bounded the western bay, and felt that he might be unequal to such exercise.

Strung along the headland was a line of round towers, which proved to be windmills, and of well-built domes, covering wells of fresh water—a source of supply for the town whence boats came to draw it. The waters of Halicarnassus were famous, in a sense infamous, in classical times. Somewhere, on or near this promontory, was the fountain of Salmacis, the source of the Hermaphrodite. The fifteen-year-old son of Hermes and Aphrodite fell in love with Salmacis and, in her waters, became 'neither man nor woman, while being something of both'. He begged of his parents that henceforward every man who bathed in the waters might lose his manly vigour, emerging with only half his sex, and to console him they granted his prayer, spreading a mysterious essence over the waters. Such is the version of Ovid.

Vitruvius, however, has a more realistic story. A Greek colonist built a tavern by the side of the spring, and the local barbarians came to drink from it, soon falling under its influence. It was not, however, the water but the society of the Greek colonists, with their gentle manner, which tamed the 'hard wild nature' of the barbarians, softening their souls with the charms of civilization.[1] On second thoughts, it might not have been inappropriate to bring my gentle friend from the milk-shop.

Before me across the water, beneath the lightening sky, the city was now revealed: twin bays, each with an arc of red-roofed houses, divided, dominated, dwarfed by the great pile of the castle, as once, on a different site, by that wonder of the world, the Mausoleum. Around me were grassy downs, smelling freshly in the aftermath of the storm. It was the fifth of November, but a few days of south-west wind and rain had brought new life to the landscape, blessing it, in a sweet second spring, with the shoots of young grass and the bloom of wild narcissi. Halicarnassus is indeed, by tradition, the land of eternal spring, and was once named Zephyria, 'from Zephyr, the wind of spring, lover of Chloris the nymph of the flowers, whose union gave birth to Carpos, the god of the fruits'.[2] Sceptically I reflected: 'If spring is here, can winter be far behind.' I left Halicarnassus on the afternoon boat. There would be none other for days to come.

* * *

Now I was back again, in a summer which indeed seemed eternal. The castle walls rose above us, gilded by the sunlight, upholstered with the grey plush leaves of a campanula, and with the rustic finery of the caper, the poor man's passion-flower. We could now wander at ease through its courtyards, laze on its battlements, gaze over an immaculate sea from its towers. Dedicated to St. Peter, the castle was built in the fifteenth century by the Knights of St. John of Jerusalem, from the island of Rhodes. Facing the sea on three sides, it covers the whole of an isthmus, which once was an island and undoubtedly the site of an ancient classical citadel. Here, as on the rock of Cnidus, the Dorians may first have maintained a footing, while the Carians still held the mainland. The knights built the castle as a footing for their raids on the Turkish mainland, and also as a refuge for Christian slaves. A race of dogs, which could distinguish the scent of a Christian from that of an

[1] Quoted by Ximinez. *op. cit.*   [2] Ximinez. *op. cit.*

infidel, sought out the slaves, in the surrounding country, and led them to the freedom of the castle.

The knights found a Turkish castle here, but demolished it. Clearly they have built on Hellenistic foundations—the familiar walls of massive mortarless stones. But using the mortar of their age, with well-faced stone, they have proved worthy enough of the masons and the craftsmen of the Greeks. As a translation of military engineering into architecture the castle is imposing enough. There is a bold simplicity in the slopes of stone, running diagonally down from the double ramparts to make a deep impregnable fosse. There is variety in the steeple-like towers and keeps, respectively manned—and perhaps built—the first by French, the second by Italian, the third by English knights. There is a confident dignity in the encircling battlements, broken only by the sea-gate, contrasting strongly with the flimsier machicolations of the Turks. Even Beaufort describes the castle as 'a far more respectable fabric than the generality of Turkish fortresses'. Newton, on the other hand, anticipating that the Turks would allow it to fall into decay, was all for pulling it down, to furnish materials for reconstruction of the harbour, but also, his mind still on the Greeks, to find evidence of the structure of the Mausoleum.

He would surely have found it. In 1522, when the knights were repairing the castle, they 'looked about for stones wherewith to make lime, and found in the middle of a level field in the port of Bodrum certain steps of marble raised in the form of a terrace'.[1] Destroying them, they dug deeper, and found themselves in a 'fine large square apartment, ornamented all round with columns of marble, with their bases, capitals, architrave, frieze and cornice engraved and sculptured in relief. The space between the columns was lined with slabs and bands of marble, ornamented with mouldings and sculpture, in harmony with the rest of the work, and inscribed in the white ground of the wall where battle-scenes were represented, sculptured in relief.' Their fancy was entertained by the singularity of the sculpture, which they paused for a moment to admire. Then they pulled it to pieces, breaking the stones up for lime. They found also a sepulchre, with a 'vase and helmet of white marble, very beautiful and of marvellous lustre'. This they had no time to open. Next day it was broken up by pirates, the earth around it left strewn with fragments of cloth of gold and spangles.

[1] Guichard. *Funérailles des Rommains, Grecs, etc.* Lyon: 1581. Quoted by Newton. *Halicarnassus, Cnidus and Branchidae.* London: 1862.

There must have been knights nevertheless who saw the beauty of this Greek work of art. For its fragments have been introduced with some care into the construction of the castle. The most substantial of these were the great frieze of the wars between the Greeks and the Amazons, and four lions' heads decorating the western rampart, which are now in the British Museum. But other traces of the classical building survive. The English tower has a Greek marble staircase, leading down to the water. The sea-gate is guarded by a headless Greek statue, of military aspect, one-legged but oddly two-footed, retrieved from the sea. Here, uniting two towers, is a wall built from a greenish polished marble; there, nicely selected, in different colours, are marble steps and plinths, a marble jamb, a marble architrave to a doorway. Here, built into the mediaeval masonry, is a stone with a Greek inscription, a scroll or a garland, part of the head of a bull; there are the marble capitals of Ionic columns, turned sideways and carved into decorative shields, with coats-of-arms. The façade of a small flamboyant chapel is carved with a Gothicized version of the classical scroll and acanthus.

Continuity in stone, between the Hellenistic Greeks and the Crusading Knights, thus persists in the castle of Halicarnassus. Moreover it is agreeable to imagine that the example of the Greeks may have inspired the knights themselves to finer craftsmanship. A wealth of heraldic sculpture decorates the castle, and this is of a quality which would not have disgraced the Mausoleum. Here, formal in character but sensitively carved and with finely-cut lettering, are the escutcheons and banners of knights and bishops, Christian insignia, armorial beasts and emblems. There, in a bold relief worthy of Eric Gill, is an effigy of St. John the Baptist, of St. Peter's Castle in miniature, of St. Peter himself with the Virgin, of knights with their ladies—and the Cross, whether of Latin or Maltese design, surmounting all. In the walls of the English tower, with its Gothic vaulting, Plantaganet knights—Sir Thomas Sheffield, John Kendal—have killed time, as they gazed across the channel towards the castle of Cos, by carving their coats-of-arms, together with the royal arms of their Sovereign, King Edward IV, and an English lion with a distinctly Mediterranean look. It was Kendal who in 1480 was sent as an emissary of the King to Ireland, to obtain aid, through indulgences, for the castle, threatened with siege by the Turks.[1] This tower alone has been damaged—by an English bombardment in the

[1] Newton. *op. cit.*

First World War. Otherwise, belying Newton's prophecies, the castle remains remarkably intact.

The Mausoleum, a Helleno-Asiatic marble tomb, a hundred and forty feet high and four hundred feet square, once dominated the western arc of the bay. In essence an Egyptian pyramid, surmounting an Ionic colonnade, it was built as a labour of grief in the middle of the fourth century B.C. by Artemisia to house the ashes of her brother and husband, Mausolus, a Hellenized Carian despot who had extended his dominion by a successful revolt against the Persians. In her despair she had previously been scenting the ashes and mixing them in her drink.[1] 'I was a tall handsome man, and formidable in war', Mausolus boasts in one of Lucian's dialogues. 'I have at Halicarnassus an immense tomb more splendid than any dead man ever had. The horses and men carved upon it are so admirably made, and in such beautiful marble, that no temple ever could be found so magnificent.'[2] It was indeed admired and spared for nearly a thousand years, by Macedonians, Romans, and Byzantines, and was only brought down by earthquakes.

Five hundred years later it was excavated by Newton—with the aid of the British Navy. In those palmy days warships were available for such leisurely pursuits as archaeology. Newton enjoyed the exclusive services of a corvette, put at his disposal by the Admiralty, with a crew of a hundred and fifty and a detachment of Sappers. Eleven years earlier, on the initiative of the Great Elchi, Lord Stratford de Redcliffe, and with the Sultan's permission, a sloop, H.M.S. *Siren*, had been despatched to Bodrum, to extract the Amazon frieze and other marbles from the walls of the castle. Its captain, Commander Harry Edgell, has left a lively diary of the operation, 'a job', as he remarks, 'quite out of our line'. The Turks looked on with some suspicion as they watched 'four jolly mariners hard at work cutting our friend [a portion of the frieze] out of the wall . . . from the anxiety of Europeans to possess what they deem worthless, they suppose them to contain some treasure'. The Commander fired a salute of twenty-one guns to the Governor, so close in to the walls that 'it sent the stone flying out, it certainly was a singular thing, and the Turks looked at each other in amazement'. The Commandant of the fortress, with a ragged set of guards who smoked on guard, and would hand a musket to a bystander on going into the village, was a man of covetous disposition: 'Everything we have on shore', writes the Commander, 'he expects to get,

[1] Ximinez. *op. cit.*

[2] Lucian. *Infer. Dialog XXIV.*

and certainly modesty forms a small part of his character, as he asks for everything, even to the pin in your shirt, he sits and sighs over small gun trucks I have on shore, as if they were children of his own.'

The gun trucks were used to transport the marbles, amid the 'wild sallies and hurrahs' of the sailors, which made the Turks smile. They were then packed in cases, made by the ship's artificer, 'sawn from the rough trees . . . and of such strength that they might be carried over the world without drama'. Halicarnassus, the Commander remarks, is 'a kind of name which Jack sadly mangles'. He himself however had an eye for the beauties of antiquity. He grows almost lyrical as he describes the marbles: 'The beauty of the countenance and perfect symmetry and roundness of limb particularly in the women, the strength of muscle in the men, with the force and energy of their positions must charm all beholders, for the living figure speaks as truly from the marble as though the whole scene were acting before us.' Commander Edgell records that the French were less successful in their efforts to see the treasures of the Castle of Bodrum. The captain of a French frigate was refused admittance, until he presented his *firman*. Then, as he was entering, the foreman 'quietly reminded him that the *firman* said nothing about his coming out again, so he must remain inside, so the poor man was as far off as ever from seeing them. On another occasion, I learnt, a visitor, with permission to "go round" the castle, was taken round the outside walls.'[1]

Newton, following the directions of Vitruvius, identified the site of the Mausoleum by means of some Ionic columns of Parian marble, lying in a field. The peasants, farming the site, quickly learnt that the Consul had found 'the Konak of some Padischah who lived two thousand years ago' and, hoping for ransom sums, made the task of excavation as hard as they could. Amongst others, he had to deal with a lady, the wife of an interested peasant, 'who looked like a first cousin of the Eumenides'. 'One day', he writes, 'when we were engaged in an experiment how near to the foundations we could venture to dig without undermining the house, a long gaunt arm was suddenly thrust through the shutters from within, and a discordant female voice screeched out some unpleasant Turkish imprecations on our heads. Mehemet Chiaoux, who happened to be standing close to the window,

[1] These extracts from the diary of Commander Edgell, afterwards Vice-Admiral Harry Edmund Edgell, are published for the first time by kind permission of Vice-Admiral Sir John A. Edgell, K.B.E., C.B.

with his back to the house, beat a hasty retreat with a very discomposed and uncomfortable expression of countenance . . . the old lady had taken the opportunity of dropping some burning cinders down his back, between his shirt and his skin.' His corporal, being a Sapper, was delighted with the discovery of underground passages. 'One day, on probing the roof of a gallery . . . he detected a soft place, and his crowbar suddenly finding its way upwards, lifted up the hearthstone of a grave sententious Turk, who was sitting quietly smoking his chibouque in his own house.' Overcoming such obstacles, Newton retrieved for the British Museum colossal statues of Mausolus and Artemisia, together with statues of lions and other busts, the remainder of the Amazon frieze, and a quantity of broken limbs which now lie on shelves in the vaults of the British Museum, as in some classical mortuary.

With the Consul-General I set off to visit the site of the Mausoleum. A fine new concrete pavement now encircled the bay, beneath a fringe of wilting palm-trees. Here and there we found relics of the former Hellenistic city: a bollard by the quayside, contrived from a fluted column, a headless statue in the municipal garden, acanthus capitals on the gate of a mosque, a kerbstone with an elaborate scroll design. Reaching the site where the Mausoleum itself once stood, we came into the garden of a tweed-capped peasant, who regarded us with blank indifference. We ferreted around in the rank dry weeds, hoping to find at least some fragment of stone, which might once have graced part of the tomb, but in vain. Where a Wonder of the World once reared its fabulous head, nothing now remains but this unkempt garden, planted with vegetable marrows and a few ragged fig-trees, enjoying an agreeable view of the sea.

CHAPTER 8

CARIA (3)

The Gulfs of the Aegean—A Week in Güllük—The Cook and the Captain—Love among the Dolphins—Tales of the Kurds—A Visitation from the North—On to the Rocks

ALONG the Aegean Coast of Turkey, between Rhodes and Samos, the sea carves its way into the land in a series of long, deep gulfs: the Doric, the Ceramic, the Mendelian. It is a seascape where the islands begin to dominate the mainland, and where indeed the mainland, with its long narrow promontories, has itself the aspect of a series of islands, making a geographical unity of the whole. But the islands are Greek and the mainland is Turkish; and though each could do with the other's merchandise there is little or no trade between them. The Turks could sell foodstuffs, tobacco and cotton, timber and hides and certain grades of stone; the Greek islanders, in return, could contribute to the Turkish economy from their minor industries of tanning, pottery, shoe-making, oil-refining, ship-building, sponge-cleaning. They could moreover be useful middlemen for the sale of such Turkish products as citrus fruits, sponges and olive-oil, which was at present limited. But there was no such commercial contact. Only in Bodrum did we find a disposition even to fraternize: a boat went across almost daily to Cos, and the Turkish harbour-master looked forward to a day when intercourse with his Greek neighbours would be freer. Some years before the *Kaymakam* had invited the Moslem 'Greeks' from Cos to Bodrum for the feast of *Bayram*. The invitation, however, was resented by the Greek authorities, who were said here to be more anti-Turkish than the Turks were anti-Greek.

To reach the head of the Mendelian Gulf, a short enough distance overland, we were obliged to do a whole day's journey by sea, down the Ceramic Gulf, round the Bodrum Peninsula, and back, following its northern shore. Here the land grows kinder, the rocks giving way to gentle hills and fertile farmsteads where orchards flourish, the cliffs to smooth, white beaches where the fruit can be easily loaded—but no longer for the barren islands opposite. The ridges are topped with round white windmills, like those of the Greeks, which once had triangular sails; the villages, with their white cubes of houses and the occasional dome of an abandoned church, are Greek in character. Here on these coasts is indeed a natural orbit of the Greeks, traditionally confirmed as such for some three thousand years, now unnaturally—but perhaps not eternally—closed even to their commerce by a recent accident of history.

Near the point of the promontory lie the ruins of Myndus, whose salted wine was so good for the digestion, with walls, here and there, which may well be Dorian, together with a classic double harbour, a landing-stage cut from the rock and a ruined fort on top of it. It was the treatment of the captain of a Myndian ship which caused a breach between Greeks and Persians, and precipitated the Ionian revolt.[1]

Turning eastwards, we reached in the evening the port of Güllük, whose name means a rose-garden. Until lately it was called Küllük, meaning an ash-heap. Here I was to stay alone for a week on the *Elfin*, while the Consul-General returned to his duties in Izmir. Güllük was a small harbour, with two or three elegant plastered house-fronts, two coffee-shops, an eating-house with room for a single table, and a public garden with whitewashed tree-trunks, adorned with a few beds of geraniums and cannas. I spent much of my time in the cleaner of the two coffee-shops, which was painted pink, with bright blue shutters, and was supervised mainly by a small boy of nine. He seldom smiled, making the coffee with swift intent concentration, serving it with an air of careful solemnity. But occasionally he would relax and with a sudden gesture fling his arms round the neck of the bovine waiter, his elder brother, who stood about all day doing nothing.

Indeed few of the characters, on the stage before me, seemed to have much to do. There was the dandy in the crimson jacket and the dark green corduroy jodhpurs, who lounged about with a swagger when the bus came in. There were the two tramp-like figures, burnt dark as negroes, who slept all day long in strange positions on upright chairs. There was the young man of Greek extraction, with large whites to his listless eyes and a crop of matted curls falling over his forehead. There

[1] Herodotus. *Book V.*

was the red-headed sailor, with a cabin-boy, who had run his uninsured caique on to a rock and lost its uninsured cargo. There was the bearded old proprietor of the eating-house, who cooked excellent fish. And there was the schoolmaster who spoke a little English. He was a sallow young man, with liquid, dissipated eyes, wearing a zipped Texas shirt, pale green trousers, a tweed jacket slung, with a studied carelessness, across his shoulders, and a broad gold wristlet watch. This I politely admired. He shrugged his shoulders and said, with an air of unexpected apology: 'It has not much gold.'

His family lived in Istanbul.

'I have six brothers,' he said, 'three men, three women'; also it seemed, two mothers, one in Istanbul, the other here.

'An aunt?' I suggested.

'Perhaps,' he said.

He had no great opinion of Güllük. Many of the people, he said, spoke not Turkish but 'Greet'.

'You mean Greek?'

'No, Greet. It is different.'

As I eventually understood, he meant Cretan. They were Turks from Crete. For most of the day he played *tric-trac*; but once he appeared with a book. It was a cheap edition of Lamb's *Tales from Shakespeare*, given to him by an English merchant seaman. His eyes brightened a little as he told me that in a few days a big English ship would come into Güllük. Such great events occurred seldom. Meanwhile the stage came to life only on certain afternoons, when the loudspeaker relayed a football match with a dramatic Turkish commentary. All gathered round to listen, making monosyllabic comments. Even the bovine waiter showed some animation, revealing himself as the local inside-right, and treating me to an assessment of the various international teams—the Hungarians, the Brazilians, the Uruguayans, the Jugoslavs, who had recently beaten the British. The Turks, he admitted, were not yet so good as these.

Most of my time was spent on board, in the company of the *Elfin's* crew. They consisted of Sadik, the Captain, and Mehmet, the cook. Sadik was a Laz with bloodshot eyes, a pink bald head and an incomplete set of teeth. He was, officially, navigator and engineer, but knew little of either of these crafts. The arrangement, I suspect, suited the Consul-General, who liked to navigate the boat and to tinker with her engines himself, and moreover to have a butt for his periodic outbursts of seafaring wrath. It suited me, feeling, as a helpless landlubber, that it might otherwise have been vented on myself. Thanks to the Captain's ineptitude, perfect harmony prevailed between myself and the Consul-General.[1]

Not so between the Captain and Mehmet, the cook, who knew better how to handle a boat than he. He was moreover a Kurd, and thus held the Captain, together indeed with most of the Turkish race, in some contempt. Mehmet was a wiry grizzled figure, with eyes which alternately laughed and sulked, an obstinate but resourceful disposition, a strong sense of the ridiculous and a certain capacity, denied to the Captain, for foresight. He cooked me excellent meals. For the first time we were well supplied with fish, which in the Mediterranean ports of Turkey is strangely hard to come by. As Mehmet cleaned it, squatting on deck, the seagulls gathered in anticipation. I could hear them, like babies, first crying, then cooing, as he flung entrails, heads and tails into the water.

The Mendelian Gulf was always rich in fish. The walled classical city of Jassus, which confronted us, just across the bay, lived largely on its fishing. Strabo tells a story of a minstrel, who was once playing the harp here before an attentive audience.[2] Suddenly the bell rang from the fish-market, and all hurried away but one. The minstrel said to him:

' "Friend, I am much obliged to you for the honour you have done me, and I admire your love of music, for all the others have left me at the sound of the bell."

' "What say you, has the bell rung?"

' "Yes," he replied.

' "Good-bye to you," said the man, and away he also went!' For he was deaf.

Athenaeus tells a romantic story of a dolphin, in the sea here at Jassus, which fell in love with a Greek boy.[3] The boy, Dionysius, with fellow-pupils of the local wrestling school, went bathing and swam out to sea. The dolphin swam up to him, took him on his back, swam a long way away with him, then set him down safely on shore. 'The dolphin', writes Athenaeus, 'is a most friendly animal to man, and extremely intelligent and knows how to repay kindness with gratitude.'

[1] He assures me, however, that Sadik's predecessor and successor were thoroughly competent.

[2] *Geography*. Book XIV.

[3] Athenaeus. *Deipnosophists*. Book XIII.

There was a man of Miletus who saved a dolphin from the fishermen; some dolphins, in return, later saved his life at Myconos; and when he died an entire school of dolphins came to his funeral.[1] Athenaeus records other such romantic attachments: a cock who fell in love with the wine-waiter of the King of Bithynia, a peacock with a girl, a goose with a boy, and another goose with a philosopher.

When fish was not available, Mehmet cooked me rice dishes with tomatoes; for the local meat, that of the goats at Milas, was notoriously bad. Standing by the cabin-door in the long striped pants which he always wore—sometimes forgetting to put his trousers on over them, when he went ashore—Mehmet, in the intervals of mocking and railing against the Captain, regaled me with tales of the refinements of cooking in his native Kurdistan, a great country, he said, for picnics. The Kurds preserved their food, throughout the lean months, by burying it under the earth floors of their homes. They made 'vintage' cheeses, spiced with garlic, which they left in the earth in pots for years, marking the date on each, and only eating the oldest. They buried meat and fruit, to dry it, and when a guest arrived all the host had to do was to take a spade and dig up the floor of the living-room: it was as good as any Frigidaire. Guinea-fowl, caught in traps, were a favourite delicacy; wild boars were shot but, in a Moslem country, never eaten; soap was made from the fat of bears; women carried miniature melons in their hands, from time to time smelling them, 'like Cologna'.

Mehmet, or so he boasted, was a man who could do anything. He could build a house, he could deliver a cow, he could mend a car. In time—indeed several times—he told me the saga of his life. His grandmother had been nurse to one of Abdul Hamid's pashas, the ruler of the country around Sirt. She had lately been killed in a motor-accident, at the age of a hundred and fifteen. His father had been a member of the Sultan's bodyguard and had left him some £5,000, most of which he lost, running successively a restaurant, a coffee-shop and other unfortunate ventures. The coffee-shop had done well enough until he painted it up and cleaned it. Then nobody came. All he now had left was £20 per month from some house-property, and another £10 from a business which he had started near Izmir, hiring out bicycles for children to ride. He came on the *Elfin*, he declared, simply to oblige the Consul-General, not because he had to, but because he

[1] Mr. Patrick Leigh Fermor has collected several such stories of dolphins, deriving from modern Greek times.

liked travelling; and he had done a good deal of it in his day. In the First World War he had fought in Kurdistan, up on the Russian frontier.

'Armenians kill plenty Kurds,' he said. 'But afterwards Kurds kill plenty Armenians.'

Finally four of his family had been killed in a single engagement. He had deserted from the Turks with four Kurdish companions. Some Kurds took them into their tent, but Mehmet did not trust them, and sat up all night with his gun between his knees, bidding his cousin do the same. Sure enough, soldiers came to arrest them, but he and his cousin escaped, while the others were hanged. They swam the Tigris in flood, but were fired at from the bank; his cousin was wounded, and he proceeded alone. After a further series of hair-raising adventures, he smuggled himself into Constantinople packed in a crate. Each evening when he grew tired of relating his adventures, Mehmet would go ashore, where he boasted that he could beat anyone in Güllük at *tric-trac*.

Early one morning, going up on deck for my before-breakfast bathe, I noticed an unfamiliar shadow across the *Elfin*, and looked up to see an apparent skyscraper, floating alongside us. It was the promised British merchantman, a new cargo-ship of ten thousand tons, so out of scale with the harbour as to reduce its houses to dolls' houses and the hills around it to molehills. Here surely was a visitation from some Cyclopean planet. For several days Güllük changed its character. There was no more fish to eat, for all the fishermen were working to load cargo—the emery stone, from the hills, used for the manufacture of grindstones, which had been accumulating in piles for some days on the quay. Loudspeakers from the ship shouted directions, snatches of Turkish song came from the stevedores, and there was a convivial atmosphere about the loading, which went on far into the night by the light of acetylene lamps. Even the women emerged, squatting happily in groups on the quays, with veils like shrouds over their heads. During the day the water splashed with an unfamiliar school of pink-and-white youths, who took a considerable interest in the *Elfin*. They hailed from all parts of their remote, northern world.

'We're quite a League of Nations on board,' said one in a Yorkshire accent which sounded curiously soft in the Aegean. 'We've chaps from London, chaps from Grimsby, chaps from Cardiff, chaps from the Clyde . . .'

I called on the Captain of the ship, a Welshman who showed me the miraculous new radar machinery, an illuminated moving 'map' of the gulf, showing every rock, with the ship herself as a pinpoint of light between them. He was in a hurry to load, because she had been delayed by the Russians and Rumanians in Constanza, the Black Sea port, of which he gave a sad picture. There was nothing to buy in the shops; vodka was ten shillings a glass in the cafés, and there was nothing else to drink but fruit syrup; the Rumanian doctors came on board, begging him for penicillin, since the Russian drugs were useless. The atmosphere of suspicion was acute. On the evening of their arrival the entire British crew were kept standing on deck for four hours, while the Communist authorities searched every cranny of the ship.

Returning to the *Elfin*, I found Mehmet cherishing, as though it were made of silver, an empty tin cigarette-box which he had got from one of the British crew and was filling with tobacco. I told him of their misadventures in Constanza. He crowed with delight.

'I like it,' he exclaimed, 'I very happy'; and he raised a glass to Malenkov.

It served us right, he explained, for sucking up to those Russians in the Second World War.

* * *

For some days the port engine had been giving trouble. The Captain proved both inept and apathetic in dealing with it. Mehmet as usual took over, dismantled the engine, found the part which he thought defective, and went to Milas, two days running, to have it repaired and fetch it back. Now all seemed to be well. We were to leave early next morning for the port of Kovela, the classical Panormus, beyond the mouth of the gulf. Thence I was to walk overland to Miletus, join the Consul-General who would be escorting the Ambassador in his Land-Rover, and return with them in the evening to the *Elfin*, visiting Heraclea and the Temple of Didyma on the way. The Captain was instructed that we must start early in the morning. By eleven o'clock he had loaded the necessary stores. Only then did he go ashore, to clear the ship's papers. Mehmet scowled, and cooked luncheon. Afterwards we set off, but the engine again gave trouble. The Chief Engineer of the British merchantman, a slow, benevolent old Scotsman, was roused from his siesta, his spry young Cockney mate was called back from a picnic, and together, without a word of resentment at their spoiled afternoons, they set the engine to rights. But it was four o'clock before we sailed. It would be hard to make Kovela by nightfall.

We crossed the gulf towards a landscape growing in scale. Higher mountains began to emerge once more on the horizon; larger villages lay spread beneath them, in the valleys of broader rivers. The Posidean promontory, where Panormus and Didyma stand, ran sharply away from them in a low flat ridge. But we were drawing back from the tail-ends of the continent into the orbit of the mainland ranges. It was dusk when we reached Karaköy, a small anchorage south of Didyma. Rather than enter Kovela in darkness, the Captain preferred to put in here for the night. But the surviving light did not prevent him from running us straight on to a reef, as he did so.

The engines, as a result of half-an-hour's effort, failed to dislodge us. The Captain stood about with an air of helpless vacancy. Mehmet, reacting to the situation with Kurdish resilience, bade him row him ashore in the dinghy. Here there was only a single building, a post of the gendarmerie. The gendarmes declared that they were not entitled to come to our assistance, and sent two small boys instead. Where the engines had failed they were hardly likely to succeed. There was nothing to do but to walk to Yeronda, the village of Didyma, two miles off, and seek assistance. Mehmet and I set off together, breathing the warm rough dusty smell of harvested crops through the darkness. As we walked, he treated me to a further instalment of his life-story. During the War of Independence he was promised a fortune of £3,000, running arms through the Greek lines to Afyon Karahissar, for the armies of Mustapha Kemal. He was caught by the Greeks and imprisoned, but made another daring escape by means of a rope given him by a Greek from Beşiktaş, the suburb on the Bosporus where he lived. He had lost his fortune and when, some years later, Atatürk's government offered him a mere few hundred pounds in compensation, he proudly refused it.

The moon was rising, and presently a high shadowed wall of massive stones loomed beside us. It was the wall of the Temple of Didyma, dwarfing the village of a punier age which now gathered around it. In its coffee-shop Mehmet turned with equal gusto from the story of his life to the story of our misfortune. After an hour's bargaining, and with the blessing of a captain of gendarmerie, who received us in his pyjamas, eight strong men, carrying telegraph poles, prepared to follow us. Led by a talkative Rumanian, who had settled here as a refugee in 1936, they were a willing crew, enjoying the walk to the sea through the balmy dusty night, and the prospect of a lira or two at the end of it. A wiry individual in a tartan shirt thumped his chest at me and exclaimed, 'Kore!' to indicate that he was a hero of Korea, then hoisted me, protesting, on to his donkey, which had a backbone like marble. The usual dandy, in a green Texas shirt with a carnation behind his ear, brought up the rear. On board the *Elfin* they removed trousers, shirts and caps, revealing shaven heads and narrow white chests and the familiar long cotton pants. One had longer hair—'Like a woman!' said a companion—but he made a crude vivid gesture to disprove it. While Mehmet commanded and the Captain ran sheepishly here and there, they scrambled into the water, and after half-an-hour of heaving and levering and tugging at ropes had us off the reef. No damage had been done and, with a series of handshakes, they left. We moved out to a safer anchorage and slept, forgetting to eat. It was already long past midnight.

CHAPTER 9

IONIA (1)

The Meander Valley—Miletus—Priene—The 'Latmic Gulf' and its Hermits—Heraclea—The Furious Eagle—Didyma—Stormy Weather in the Straits—Farewell to the 'Elfin'

EARLY NEXT MORNING we put into Kovela, and I set off on a three hours' walk to the great classical city of Miletus. Here was a soft Ionian landscape, fringing a gentle sea. Arcadian fields of golden stubble gleamed in the early sunlight; spreading fruit-trees, figs and pomegranates relieved them with pools of shade; the hedgerows romped with wild blue thistles, hollyhocks and brambles. As I walked, the fertile land ebbed away into a wild arboretum, where arbutus and juniper bloomed in the sand between shingly beaches and slopes of scented lavender. Ahead of me mountains bestrode the sky with an easy arrogance. The coast-line grew rockier, but still made way for inlets and bays of cultivation, where women in yellow kerchiefs stacked the grain or picked the tobacco. They were a taciturn people, who gave me barely a greeting as I passed.

Laboriously—for my sandals were falling to pieces, and had at intervals to be patched with 'Elastoplast'—I was approaching the Latmic Gulf of classic geography, the Meander plain of today. A last ascent—or so I hoped it to be—lay before me. At the top of it was the village of Ak Köy, boasting a silvered bust of Atatürk and a whitewashed mosque, with plaster columns fluted in the classical manner. Here a gendarme greeted me with a message that the Consul-General's Land-Rover was on its way to pick me up. I was glad of the lift, now noticing that yet another ridge lay ahead, and my 'Elastoplast' was finished. Surmounting it, we soon saw, spread beneath us, the broad Meander valley, and beyond it the lordly range of Mount Mycale sweeping up from a distant sea.

Here, as today in the Doric, the Ceramic and the Mendelian Gulfs, the sea once penetrated far into the land. Here, on the other hand, a great meandering river was to change the course of geography—the river whose channel was said to inscribe the entire Greek alphabet.[1] The Meander winds for two hundred and fifty miles to do the hundred and fifty from source to mouth. In Strabo's time landowners sued it in the courts, for removing their fields and demolishing their boundaries, and its fines were paid from the proceeds of its ferries. As time went on the silt which it brought down from the Phrygian highlands filled up the Latmic Gulf, engulfing islands and isolating ports bigger than either Halicarnassus or Cnidus. By the nineteenth century Fellows (who compared its wanderings, rather prosaically, to those of the river at Stirling) was prophesying that 'the recent earth, now soft, will harden, and the present marshes be dry. The shore will in time protrude so far that . . . it will unite with Samos, and in a series of years extend to remoter islands . . . Some barren rock of the adjacent deep may be enriched with a fertile domain, and other cities rise and flourish from the bounty of the Meander.'

The bounty has not yet extended so far. Hard earth however does now cover the gulf; moreover it is at times so dry that, where a few years ago men were propping up the river's banks, now on the contrary they are breaking them down, that the land may be irrigated. Less than a generation ago this plain was still largely a marsh, 'covered with tall grass and riddled with lagoons . . . lair of wild boars and countless aquatic birds'.[2] Much of it remained derelict until the end of the Second World War, while the remainder was mere rough seasonal grazing for the nomadic shepherds of the plateau. Today it stretched before me as busily cultivated as the delta of the Nile. The irregular stutter of a tractor drifted across it from rich brown cotton-fields, now encroaching on a patchwork of maize and yellowing pasture. But the weather of the plain remains the weather of the sea. A sea-mist still rises from it, early in the morning. Fellows describes here an 'awful night of successive storms of thunder'. The sou'-westerly winds grant little mercy to the reclaimed land, sweeping dramatically across it, with curtains of rain cloud, as though to whip up the waves which once were there. When first I came to Miletus, three years before, the clouds, with full orchestra of thunder and lightning, had staged an all-day operatic performance, throwing a drop-curtain down over the opposite

[1] George Wheler. *A Journey into Greece*. London: 1682.

[2] Ximinez. *op. cit.*

shore whence we had come, but leaving us dry in the sunlight with a grandstand view of the deluge. Returning at night we had to flounder for hours through a morass, to which the land had now reverted.

But today all, beneath the midday sun, was serene. The Consul-General, with the Ambassador, greeted me from the summit—the fifty-fourth row—of the theatre. Built largely of marble, weathered, rugged and red, it is the largest in Asia Minor: a substantial pile, rising like an architectural mountain above the plain on supporting walls and vaults of Roman masonry. Before us, beyond the elaborate proscenium, was a battered Turkish *han*, and here, as though for our benefit, a continuous scene was being enacted by a company of cotton-pickers, Turkish refugees from Bulgaria. The women, in bright flowing kerchiefs and billowing trousers, walked with a natural dignity and disputed with lively gestures. The children swarmed over the roof, where bright-coloured laundry lay spread out to dry in the sun, playing games, quarrelling, arranging posies of wild flowers in frames of broken marble. Suddenly a policeman, in top-boots and breeches, swept on to the scene like some dark and menacing Tricorne, and with the arm of authority silenced and scattered them, ordering the children off the roof and setting the women to work, sweeping the courtyard.

Miletus was the Meander's principal victim. Colonized by Ionians from the evacuated lands of Attica, in about the tenth century B.C., it enjoyed a long supremacy in the Ionian League which was largely due to its naval wealth and power. Situated on the gulf, near the mouth of the Meander, with four convenient harbours, it commanded not only the seas around it but the land route behind it, up into the heart of Asia Minor. Its commerce thus flourished, and its seafaring people founded as many as eighty colonies—more, it is said, than any other classical city—extending from the Black Sea right to the Atlantic. Unlike other Ionian cities, Miletus remained strong enough through the centuries to resist conquest by the powers of the interior, with whom it formed alliances. In the arts and sciences it became, in a sense, the Athens of Asia Minor. 'Never within so narrow a space', wrote the Abbé Barthélemy of this corner of Asia Minor, 'did Nature produce so great a number of men of destiny, talents and sublime genius.'[1] And Miletus for centuries wore the crown. The Milesians were finally defeated by the Persians, following the Ionian Revolt during the reign of Darius, when the Greek fleet was defeated off the island of Lade,

[1] Abbé Barthélemy. *Travels of Anacharsis the Younger in Greece*. London: 1817.

before the city. The Athenians were so affected by this catastrophe that, when the play of 'The Capture of Miletus' was given on the stage, the audience burst into tears, stopped the performance and caused Phrynicus, the author, to be fined a thousand drachmae. Later, thanks to the victory of the Athenians in the Battle of Mycale, Miletus gained a new lease of life, under their influence. It was still a powerful city at the time of Alexander, who equally besieged it from Lade. It was nature, not man, that defeated it. The sea slowly ebbed from the city until it ceased to be a port; its four harbours became totally silted up, until not even a channel connected it with the sea; and today Lade, together with five other islands, is a mere hump-backed hillock, rising up from the plain.

From the top of the theatre we looked down over the city, now overgrown with scrub, but conforming still in its ruins to a grandiose classical plan. Here, lined by sumptous public buildings—town hall, customs house, baths, gymnasia—is a wealth of spacious streets and markets befitting a city which, even in Roman times, continued to thrive—if no longer supreme—on its trade. Its solid Roman quays still line the fields where the principal harbour lay, and it is easy to imagine the ships sailing into it, between two colossal stone lions, which guarded the entrance.[1] Ahead, dominating the business quarter, was the triumphal victory monument; to the left of the harbour the temple of the Delphinian Apollo, the patron of sailors; farther inland the Nymphaeum, half sanctuary, half public garden, with its monumental fountain; to the right an imposing circular monument, whose purpose remains obscure. Scrambling laboriously through the city, we identified the landmarks, regretting only that no herd of goats accompanied us, to devour the thick undergrowth which may otherwise envelop the excavations, restoring them once more to oblivion.

Miletus, with its dwindling Byzantine trade, survived to be conquered by the Turks, and indeed one of its finest monuments is a Seljuk mosque, standing amid aged trees in a secluded restful courtyard. Its façade is of marble, built from the stones of the city, re-polished and re-fashioned to suit the oriental design. Its minaret, when we saw it, was crowned with a stork's nest; its tiled, brown dome well thatched with golden mosses. Within, it was a graceful canopy of swirling brickwork, pointed in the Persian style. The mosque had fallen into disuse. Little life survives in Miletus today but that of the

[1] Félix Sartiaux. *Villes Mortes d'Asie Mineure*. Paris: 1911.

storks, building their nests on the roofs and in the stunted trees of the somnolent village of Balat—a name, meaning, ironically, Palaces.

* * *

Miletus, even in ruins, is a Metropolis. Priene, on the opposite 'bank' of the Meander plain, is its direct antithesis, the small city-state. Both were colonized at the same period by Ionians. But whereas the one grew rich and powerful, holding its own with its enemies and spreading its influence abroad, the other remained modest, unambitious, submitting with dignity to its enemies, content to live its own life within its own walls. This life, however, was vivid enough. Priene was a city devoted less to commerce and war than to religion, to sport, to culture, indeed to the arts of living.

Priene ceased to be a port before Miletus: by Strabo's time it was already forty stadia from the sea.[1] I had visited it three years before from Söke, the cotton 'boom town' of the new Meander plain, which boasted a thousand new tractors, several new millionaires, and many thousands of small peasants become newly-rich landowners. They had reason to be grateful to the Earth goddess, Demeter, worshipped by the people of Priene, for a crop she never knew. The classical bay-tree still graces the ruins of her shrine, whence I looked down into gardens now smoking with the olive boughs and flaming with the fig-leaves of a mellowing autumn. Priene sits on the grassy lap of a lower slope of Mount Mycale, with a cliff behind it like the long straight back of a throne, and with walls still around it, recalling its former gentle aloofness.

Hellenistic in style, unpretentious in scale, Priene has a refined simplicity which few cities of Greece can equal. The theatre, with its mere eight rows of seats in contrast to the fifty-four at Miletus, with its elegant armchair stalls for honoured visitors, with its simple pillared proscenium and its marble altar of Dionysus, conveys the intimacy of the early Greek drama, as opposed to the more lavish popular spectacles of later days. The intimate council chamber, with its marble altar and its three surmounting blocks of seats, still rings in imagination with the order and enlightenment of Greek debate. The market square, compact and sociable, surrounded by marble shops, furnished with the marble slabs of fishmongers, still seems to echo with the bargaining and the gossip and the talk of Greek citizens, bent on

[1] *Geography*. Book XIV.

their everyday activities. The gymnasium, with its changing room and oiling room and sanding room, its wash-room fitted with marble basins and lion-headed taps, above all its names of students scratched on the walls, recaptures the spirit of Greek youth, Greek health and vigour.

But it is Priene's residential quarter which brings the city most vividly to life. The streets, built on a grid-plan at varying levels, are long and wide, with marble paving and marble steps at the side. The houses, as can be seen from their walls and foundations, were small but spacious, filled with light, their rooms giving on to an interior courtyard, their walls stuccoed and painted with decorative designs. Above all, from a profusion of runnels and fountains tapping the springs of Mount Mycale, they enjoyed the comforts of running water in every room. In the harmony, the intimacy, the *douceur de vivre* of Priene lies the essence of Ionia, the essence of ancient Greece itself.

* * *

A stretch of the Latmic Gulf survives in the form of an inland lake: Lake Bafa. Its waters, now sweet with a touch of salt, and enriched with alluvial mud, drain into the Meander through a narrow canal. Here fish from the sea pass up into the lake to spawn and back to feed, sleek grey mullet, whose forbears graced the table of Themistocles.[1] Across the outlet, at Dalyan, the Turks have built bamboo cages to catch them. We watched as they fished them out with long landing-nets, then flung them on the concrete floor of a shed, to perform a demented dance of death. Strong and powerful as they were, the fish died hard, dancing on head, then on tail with a frenzy of twists and jumps for some minutes on end; but the men assured us indifferently that they felt nothing. Here a station has been built to freeze and cure them, for export abroad and to other parts of Turkey. Their roes go to Greece, by boat from Kovela, to make *tarama*, the favourite delicacy of Greek *tavernas*. The conger-eels from the lake once went to Germany, by boat via Trieste. Now they go instead to Holland. The concession, a monopoly in the hands of a prosperous landowner from Söke, is a rich one.

One of his sons now entertained us to a luncheon beginning with salted eels and *raki*. In the heat of the day this mixture hardly quenched our thirst, but it was varied, until the arrival of the mullet, by a profusion of pears and apricots. Afterwards our host, a young *effendi* with

[1] Chandler. *op. cit.*

a moustache and spectacles, who took turns with his brother to run the station, drove us to the lake where a caique awaited us. Here the shallows were such that we had to take a punt to reach it. For the Meander's invasion continues, wresting land from the water, thrusting out armies of reeds like an advance guard, to conquer its surface. Where yesterday our hosts fished, today they plough. But the lake is still ten miles long. As we sailed slowly up it several fish jumped right over the boat, while pelicans watched from the rocks, taking off like clumsy flying-boats, with necks outstretched, to pursue them.

'Those birds are our rivals,' said the *effendi*, letting off his rifle ineffectively. We came upon a dead tree laden with cormorants, coarse ornaments of jet burdening filigree branches, and he fired his rifle once more, dispersing the birds, destroying the picture.

As history progressed the Latmic Lake, sealed in not only by its encircling mountains but by the encroaching marshes of the Meander valley, derived new life from its very isolation. 'When monkery', writes Chandler, 'spreading from Egypt towards the end of the fourth century, overran the Greek and Latin Empires', it became a retreat for the Christians. 'The lake,' he writes, 'abounding in large and fine fish, afforded an article of diet not unimportant under a ritual which enjoined frequent abstinence from flesh', and it was 'a grand resort of fanciful devotees and secluded hermits, a nursery of saints, another Athos, or holy mountain'. It may well have remained so until the mediaeval incursions of the infidel. Its islands are ringed with the walls of Byzantine monasteries, 'fortresses' looking inwards, as those of the Greeks had looked outwards. Their stonework, alternating with brick, is rough but solid enough to have endured, through decay, for a thousand years. Here is a chapel intact, now adopted as a stable by goats; there a buttressed arch, still carrying walls, unbroken, across a cleft in the rock. On either hand mountains close in on the lake in a pandemonium of granite slabs and monoliths, strangely smooth, yet so colossal as to seem immune from human approach. Grimmer and more passively hostile than the neighbouring limestone ranges, these crags have yet been breached by many thousands of cells and tombs, where monks, inspired perhaps by the preachings of the followers of St. Paul at Miletus, came to live in seclusion, and where their bones now lie.

Over all presides the black lunar summit of Mount Latmus, where Endymion slept and was embraced, as its rocks still are, by the moon.

Strabo records that his sepulchre was to be seen here, in a cave.[1] Beneath this peak, by a beach of powdered marble, the ruined port of Heraclea survives, its immaculate Greek walls rebuking, as it were, the unruly boulders around it. Built on terraces, linked by steps cut into the rock, are the relics of a theatre, of an *agora*, of a temple, of a serene upstanding tower, commanding the ruined fortifications. On a beach nearby, looking vigilantly across the lake, is a Turkish or Genoese fort, imposing enough until it is seen to be but a single wall—an unconscious 'folly'.

Returning to the fish-curing station, we sat in the well-kept modern farmyard, refreshing ourselves with long cool draughts of cherry-juice. Peasant retainers served us, sprinkling water on the ground beneath our feet to lay the dust. Around us livestock abounded. Horses, proud as those of the breed of Troy, tossed their heads in the stable. Storks, like old-age pensioners, stood sentry in their nests on the rooftops. A group of cygnets, skinny as children, splashed in an ordinary bath let into the ground, caged-in by netting. The father of our host intended them as a gift, perhaps to Celal Bayar, the President, perhaps to the public gardens in Izmir. We were presented with a nest full of purple young fledglings, which a cat had just brought in. Then one of the retainers brought us a full-grown eagle, with a fierce yellow beak, 'one of those dusky hunters whose colour calls to mind the ripening grape' [2] but which had broken its wing and was thus condemned to eternal captivity. He carried the proud bird with a careless indifference, as though it were no more than a hen, while it struggled and croaked and scowled at its fate, with a glare of furious humiliation in its eye. Our host had little taste for such rustic surroundings. He was hankering for the bright lights of Söke, beyond the Meander.

For our part we were anxious to reach Didyma, the great temple of Apollo, before dark. Didyma was the Delphi of Asia. Its founder was Branchus, either the son, the descendant or the beloved of Apollo. His name meant Throat, and he was given it because his mother, while pregnant, saw the sun pass down her throat and into her womb. Endowed by Apollo with the gift of prophecy, he built the temple in his honour and called it the Didymaeon, either from the twins loved by Apollo, or from a neighbouring mountain with twin summits. His descendants, the Branchidae, remained its hereditary priests until the temple's destruction by Xerxes after the Battle of Salamis. They are

[1] *Geography*. Book XIV. [2] *Iliad*. Book XXIV.

said to have ceded to him the treasures of the temple, and then accompanied him to Persia. There, in revenge for their perfidy, the armies of Alexander massacred their descendants, and the oracle was revived, acquiring a new lease of life and bringing valuable revenue to Miletus.

The Milesians planned the new temple on so vast a scale that they were never able to finish it. Even so it must have been worthy to rank as an eighth Wonder of the World. They worked at it for a hundred and fifty years, deriving funds from various sources. With the fall of Miletus the work lapsed for a century; it was resumed by Caligula, only to lapse again under Hadrian. The oracle continued into Christian times, while Christian chapels grew up around it. It survived even the raids of pirates. Its disappearance was gradual. The unfinished temple was still standing in the fifteenth century, when an Italian, Cyriacus of Ancona, saw it. Its final destruction was due to an earthquake, at the end of the century.

Even in ruins, the temple of Didyma reduces the surrounding village to Lilliputian proportions. Stepped high on its ample marble platform, within spacious precincts, massively walled, it achieves, for all its immensity, dignity of stature and refinement of design. Its two surviving Doric columns, soaring skywards to a height of sixty-four feet, are so moulded and fluted as to convey a sense of lightness and grace. Lower only than those of the smaller Roman Temple of Baalbek, and by a mere six inches, they stand poised at the head of the broad surrounding stairway, and are thus in fact a hundred feet from the ground. A double rank of these mighty columns lined three sides of the temple, flanking deep thick marble walls, of a prison-like severity, appropriate to the mysteries within. Only these two, together with a simpler Ionic column, still remain intact, and indeed some may never have been erected; but several lie just as the earthquake felled them, spreading their majestic length on the ground. A broad shallow staircase, broken by two great pediments designed for statues, leads up to the portico of the temple and to the *pronaos*, an outer hall of columns of which some had capitals adorned with busts of the gods, and the drums of others still stand on bases finely carved in relief with floral and scroll designs. Lying on the ground below is the gigantic head of a winged Medusa, a survivor of the frieze which once surmounted them.

This vestibule is but a fourth part of the temple, which stretches away to a vast marble hall beyond it. But it was all that the bulk of the pilgrims saw. The rest was sacred, hidden behind a great blank wall, still standing, with a lofty door six feet above the ground and habitually closed, but for the emergence of the priest in certain ceremonies. Its threshold is the hearthstone of the temple, a marble monolith twenty-seven feet long and sixty tons in weight. To hear the words of the oracle, the favoured pilgrims went down one of the two narrow corridors, still intact, on either side of it: steep marble tunnels, too narrow to allow more than a single person to pass, but flawlessly built, their walls and vaulting faced and jointed with the harmony of art, and the signatures of their craftsmen carved on bosses which project from the walls. From an open chamber above it a broad stairway, for the priests alone, descends into the *naos*, the main hall of the temple, a vast 'double cube', open to the sky, where the giant statue of Apollo stood and the prophetesses practised their mysteries, received their gifts and propounded their oracles. Strabo [1] records that, on account of its size, it remained without a roof. More probably either the Milesians had been unable to pay for a roof, or, as Texier suggests, it was intended to be an open courtyard.

In its scale, in its construction, in the quality of its sculpture, the Temple of Didyma epitomizes the flowering of a style more monumental, because more Asiatic, than that of the temples of Greece, but like them derived from the will to create, to achieve, through infinite pains and experiment, perfection. Justly did Chandler exclaim: 'The columns yet entire are so exquisitely fine, the marble mass so vast and noble, that it is impossible perhaps to conceive greater beauty and majesty of ruin'. The Turks, though they preserve the temple, are not, perhaps, altogether responsive to its beauty. In the centre of the *naos*, before the sacred staircase, the villagers had sunk a well, as large as a pond, fitted with a clumsy paraphernalia of boards and ropes and pulleys. This had been done, so they assured us, by permission of the Minister of Public Instruction—'for the water is sweet'. Their village looked insignificant in the twilight, as we took a last look at the temple, its marble columns bathed in a dull grey glow.

From here to the sea at Panormus ran a Sacred Way, by which the pilgrims approached the temple. It was lined with statues, of which Newton found the survivors: a lion, a sphinx, and a number of figures seated in chairs. On one of these he found an inscription, 'I am Chares, son of Klesis, ruler of Teichioussa; an offering to Apollo', enabling him to date it to about 520 B.C., and suggesting that it might be the oldest

[1] *Geography*. Book XIV.

Greek portrait statue known. He detected Egyptian influence in the statues, perhaps confirming the tradition that early Greek sculptors, from Asia Minor, studied their art in Egypt. We saw nothing of the Sacred Way, or indeed of its statues, since Newton removed them to the British Museum, where they sit today. A parallel modern road took us to Panormus, the Kovela which I had left early that morning. After a hot and weary day we looked forward to a drink, a dinner cooked by Mehmet, and a sound night's rest, chugging gently northwards on board the *Elfin*.

In the last we were disappointed. All day long a strong wind had been blowing from the West. On setting sail the Captain ran us once more on to the mud, from which however the Consul-General, with some adroitness, dislodged us. But outside the harbour we soon ran into a boisterous sea. All night long, as the *Elfin* struggled northwards with a creaking of its timbers and a shuddering of its frame, the Ambassador and I lay tossing wakefully, side by side, in our bunks, each pretending to the other that we slept heedlessly through it all. The Consul-General meanwhile, a looming figure in pyjamas, swayed at the tiller, shouting orders and imprecations at the Captain, a little anxious no doubt when the port engine failed for an hour or so, but otherwise plainly in his element. At first light, shedding pretence, I put on a sweater and stood precariously in the stern, enjoying the buffets of the balmy morning gale and the salt spray thrashing across my cheeks.

We were pitching now through the narrow Straits of Samos, as sailors must have done in such a wind since the days of the Achaeans, watching this same eternal sun-dried landscape, where the continent with a flourish gives way to the islands. To the east Mount Mycale, the extremity of Asia's great land mass, swept down to the promontory of the Panionion, where the Ionian cities from earliest times came together to do honour to the Sea God. Here a thousand years later came St. Paul, landing on the promontory as he travelled from Troy to Miletus, heralding a new civilization, with the cult of a new Sea God, St. Nicholas. Above St. Paul's Harbour, where the relics of chapels but not of temples survive,[1] the sun now rose from behind the sacred mountain, a liquid disc, with a dull glow of flame, ready to warm the land once more. In the surging channel an island with a lighthouse flushed suddenly gold with light, while the coastguards waved us a greeting with a red Turkish flag. Behind them rose the low baked hills

[1] Ximinez. *op. cit.*

of Samos, a white Greek town, with an ancient fortress, hugging its stormbound shores.

The wind subsided as we passed through the Straits, and I returned to my bunk. After two hours' sleep I awoke to a miraculous calm. The *Elfin* at last lay at anchor. The sun was already well up in the sky, and from across the water rang the unbroken melodious voice of a boy, singing with all his might. I looked out to see a landscape terraced and planted with well-pruned olives, above a hamlet of clean white houses. This was Greek land. The Consul-General had brought us into a sheltered cove of Samos, and presently the boy, still singing, drew alongside in a boat, to converse with a lively Greek curiosity. Having breakfasted and bathed we tossed into a kindlier wind across the broad Cayster Gulf, to make landfall off the ancient port of Colophon, its tall white cliffs falling into submarine canyons, which we explored with our heads under water. In the afternoon, half drugged by a heat like a sirocco and by the fatigue due to our sleepless night, we walked inland in slow motion, to the ruins of Claros, a place renowned for the cult of Apollo since the time of the Trojan War. French archaeologists had lately uncovered a Doric temple, with inscriptions dating from the third century B.C., and I had seen its columns two years earlier, neatly packed and preserved in silt, just as they lay after the earthquake had brought them to the ground. But now the ruins were flooded with water, which seeped up into them each winter, hampering further excavation.

For the night we lay off Lebedos, once the centre of the Ionian theatrical profession, of which only some traces of Hellenistic wall survive. More remains of Teos, nearby: massive stones overgrown with a tangle of fig and wild olive, against a background of dry pink hills and a lively blue sea. Its ruins were excavated and recorded in a series of engravings by the Dilettanti Society, who refer to a beautiful portico of the Temple of Bacchus, 'erected at the seat of the Right Hon Lord Despenser, in High Wycomb . . . in which the exact proportions of the order are observed'. From here we walked across a neck of land to Siğacik, a neat somnolent port within Byzantine walls, which marked the end of our voyage on the *Elfin*. Soon we were driving along a tarmac road, through parks of valona oak, towards Smyrna.

CHAPTER 10

IONIA (2)

Smyrna and Izmir—The Frankish Merchants—Ephesus—Artemis and St. Paul—Modern Cult of the Virgin—Celebrations in Selcuk

SMYRNA, until a generation ago, was a lively cosmopolitan port. Pococke, in the eighteenth century, wrote that 'the great number of Franks who are settled there make Smyrna a very agreeable place, and there is no want of good company, they live in a very sociable manner, and are particularly civil to strangers'. Hamilton, in the nineteenth, enjoyed the gay costumes in the bazaars 'from the heterogeneous nations that swarm and congregate in this busy quarter'.[1] Davis describes 'many a brilliantly painted café, projecting into the sea on piles', but complains of the lack of an open space or a public promenade. Smyrna was burnt and the Greeks driven out of it in 1922. Rebuilt as Izmir, it seems to be all open spaces, all public promenades. Its centre is today a vast Kültür Park, with concrete paths and an artificial lake. Few cafés adorn the front, whose principal place of entertainment is a single neon-lit cabaret. Here Turks in their shirt-sleeves, with stolid expressions, watch the antics of a few girls, imported no longer from Hungary but from Italy and France, and of the Consular Corps and the N.A.T.O. officers, as they decorously dance after dinner. Izmir is a sterilized city, no longer cosmopolitan, no longer picturesque, but worthily, busily Turkish.

A trace of Greek atmosphere lingers in the elegant suburb of Bornova, where the survivors of the 'Frankish' merchants live in ample nineteenth-century villas amid lawns and flower-beds and flowering trees. The Greeks have gone, and with them the lively social and cultural life which Bornova once enjoyed. But other prosperous merchant families, British and French, remain: the Forsytes of the Levant living, much as their fathers and grandfathers did, on the comforting proceeds

[1] W. J. Hamilton. *Researches in Asia Minor*. London: 1852.

of trade. The Consul-General lived among them, and I relaxed in his house with a sense of solid well-being. Around us the storks and their young, nesting in the treetops and chimney-pots, gave an air of domesticity to the gardens. Of respectability too: I was assured by a neighbour that the stork is a monogamous bird, with rigid views on marital fidelity, who returns each year to the same nest, with the same wife. Lately, in a neighbour's garden, when an impish child put a turkey's egg in the place of a stork's egg in a nest, the stork community massed around its mistress and did her to death.

In the old days of Smyrna few of these merchant clans spoke Turkish. Now, to keep pace with the times, they learn the language, and bring Turks into their firms as partners. Once eighty per cent of the trade of Smyrna was in foreign hands; now ninety per cent of it is in Turkish hands. The Turk, unlike the Greek, has no natural aptitude for commerce: the military rather than the business mind pervaded the Atatürk régime. Today, under the Democrats, he is learning its mysteries. But he remains reluctant to invest and requires foreign capital, which in the past he mistakenly spurned. Dried fruits are Izmir's stock-in-trade. Its raisin and fig Bourse has a stateliness worthy of the Bank of England, the merchants in their cubicles displaying their wares with solemnity in carefully graded sample heaps. Wheat was once the staple crop. After the departure of the Greeks and the arrival of Turks from Bulgaria and Macedonia, tobacco began to take its place. It flourishes still: the Turks maintain that they can produce not merely a Turkish but a Virginian tobacco as good as the American, and with less 'sauce' in it. Today, however, the 'boom' crop is cotton, which enriches merchants, landowners and peasants alike.

Izmir, steaming at the head of its long sultry Gulf, owes its prosperity, foretold by the oracle of Claros, to a sheltered natural harbour, and its site to a dream of Alexander the Great. While he slept under a plane tree on the slopes of Mount Pagus, the goddess Nemesis gave him certain specific instructions, and the city was afterwards built where he had lain. Its harbour needs constant dredging, and might well have become silted up at the mouth, like that of Miletus. But late in the nineteenth century the Turks, with the aid of German engineers, changed the course of its river Gediz (the Hermus), distributing the alluvial wealth of Phrygia elsewhere and extending its lease of life, perhaps, for some further centuries. The earlier city of Smyrna, called after an Amazon, stood to the north-west of Izmir, beyond the warm

Baths of Diana where pagans worshipped, Christians performed baptisms and Turks deposit chemical waste. It is claimed, together with numerous other cities, as the birthplace of Homer, and Chandler pretends to have found the cave where the poet wrote his verses. Small and compact as a village, the old city descends in layers to a set of foundations which may date from 900 B.C., and its polygonal Greek masonry, closely jointed, is among the earliest known.

The later classical city took full advantage of the mountain, with its protective ridges, its ample slopes and its rich supplies of marble. Successively the Greeks, 'studious to unite beauty with strength and good ports with a fertile soil', and the Romans 'ever attentive to articles neglected by them, to the paving of the ways, to the building of aqueducts and to the common shores',[1] made Smyrna 'the crown of Ionia', 'the ornament of Asia'. Aristides describes it as a city 'putting forth continually the bloom of its age, like a city that was not built by slow degrees but once and for all rose from the ground'.[2] From the Acropolis 'everything as far as the shore is a blaze of gymnasia, markets, theatres, precincts, harbours, where natural and man-made beauties vie with each other, baths so many that you would not know where to bathe, public walks of every kind . . . fountains and running waters for each house and more . . . the delights of the soul never desert it'. A diversion of the city was the persecution of Christians: the crowds in its stadium called for a lion, to tear St. Polycarp to pieces. The official in charge, being well-disposed towards him, refused, and they were allowed instead to burn him. He is remembered still, beside the crumbling walls of a Byzantine fortress.

Little of all this classical glory remains, except part of the *agora* on the hillside, with monumental statues of Poseidon and Demeter, and a network of underground shops and corridors, their vaulting ribbed and crossed in such a manner as to foreshadow the Gothic. In the museum in the Kültür Park the bearded Roman God of the Meander reposes in voluptuous ease, with a wreath of flowers in his hair and a cornucopia in his arms, overflowing with pineapples, pomegranates, grapes and other fruits of the valley—but not yet its cotton or tobacco.

* * *

Smyrna never quite rivalled Ephesus, a city 'filled with studious people, both philosophers and rhetoricians', that 'grew in size beyond

[1] Chandler. *op. cit.* [2] Aristides. *Book XVII.*

all other cities of Ionia and Lydia'.[1] We drove to it in comfort along the tarmac road, touching the coast at Kuşadasi, a mere half-town since the burning of its Greek half, looking across from a beach, devoid of bathers, to a castle on an island and the hump of Samos beyond. Ephesus, like Miletus, is cut off from the sea—this time by the Little Meander. Thus, unlike Smyrna, much of it survives in ruin. From an amphitheatre of rough blue hills, its bay lay spread like an arena beneath us, its waters stained at the river's mouth by a tell-tale crescent of mud, its roadstead filled with a half-moon of land, where camels grazed on soft pink mosses. Here is no landlocked trough, like the harbour of Smyrna, but a broader, windswept gulf, swayed by the varying moods of the Aegean. In a north wind it sulks, in a west wind it rages, in an east wind it scintillates, lucid and clear, the walls of Colophon moving sharply into focus beyond it.

Where the camels now graze a fair wind brought St. Paul, sailing in a galley from Corinth, up the channel and into the harbour of Ephesus. The quay where he landed, the baths where travellers washed off the grime of the journey, now peter out into a marshy wilderness. But the street up which he walked, from the harbour to the city, survives, twelve yards broad and paved with marble, revealing traces of a colonnade, of statues, of porticoes, befitting a triumphal avenue. It culminates in the theatre, hewn from one of the twin hills which mark the site of the city, a place designed on a sumptuous scale, no longer for the intimate Greek drama but for the lavish Roman spectacle. Its audiences—at least in the upper rows—had much to distract them from the scene, since the centre of Ephesus, compact for all its grandeur, lay, as its ruins still lie, visibly spread beneath them.

There, at the foot of long and crowded avenues, was the harbour, crowded with shipping. Here, at the head of it, is the gymnasium with its spacious courtyards, where they could watch the youth of the city at its sports. To the left another marble street, hardly less wide than the first, with vaulted drains beneath it, leads to the *agora*, the bazaar where the merchants traded in an opulent Roman setting, beneath a wealth of imperial inscriptions. Adjoining it stands the public library, a retreat well suited, by contrast, to the affairs of the mind. Its calm harmonious reading-room, once paved with mosaic and adorned by statues of Wisdom, Virtue, Fortune and Knowledge, gives on to a marble courtyard. Its shelves are let into the walls, by a practical municipality, in

[1] Aristides. *Book XXIII.*

such a way as to protect the books against damp, and raised on a surrounding marble ledge to protect them against dirt and damage. Between them is a niche for the statue of Celsus, the Roman senator and Governor-General of Asia, whose heirs built the library in his honour; marble panels, on the walls, were inscribed with his biography in Latin and Greek; and his body lies in a marble sarcophagus, adorned with garlands, beneath the library—a resting-place becoming to any scholar or patron of literature. To the right of the theatre, quarried out of the hillside, a stadium, as big as a pair of football fields, looks out over the plain where the city's leading industry once stood: the Temple of Artemis, that Diana of the Ephesians whom St. Paul was to challenge and eventually defeat.

The Ephesian cult of Artemis dates back to a pre-Hellenic period. It was adopted from the indigenous Asiatic population by the Ionian colonists, who set apart a month each year for the festival of the Artemision. Originally the goddess's image was a block of wood, perhaps of vine, believed by her devotees to have fallen from the skies as a gift from Jupiter, and endowed with a multiplicity of pendent breasts, to denote fertility. It survived decay thanks to treatment with a brand of nard, which preserved its humidity. The priesthood of the cult consisted of eunuchs and well-bred virgins. The temple is said to have been re-built seven times, starting as the mere hollow trunk of a tree with the image inside it, and rising eventually to be one of the Seven Wonders of the World. The sixth-century temple, to which Croesus contributed golden heifers, was spared by Xerxes, alone among the shrines of Ionia, but burnt down by a madman called Herostratus on the night, as it happened, that Alexander the Great was born. He aspired, it seems, to perpetuate his name: an objective ensured by the general assembly of the States of Ionia, who passed a decree consigning it to oblivion. Alexander offered to rebuild the temple, but the Ephesians tactfully declined, suggesting that it was unbecoming for one god to erect temples to others. Instead they rebuilt it themselves, employing as an architect Dinocrates, who had intended carving the whole of Mount Athos into a statue of Alexander. The ladies of Ephesus contributed their jewels to help finance the work. It was four times the size of the Parthenon; its folding gates were of cypress 'treasured up for four generations, highly polished' and 'continued four years in glue', so that four hundred years later they were fresh as new; the ceiling was of cedar; the steps to the roof were of a single stem of a vine; and the altar was carved by Praxiteles. It was a prosperous concern. The goddess owned valuable estates in the Cayster valley, together with quarries, pastures, salt-pans and fisheries. The temple became also a kind of bank, where citizens, taking advantage of its right of asylum, deposited their money and other valuables, and sums were loaned on note of hand. The silversmiths of Ephesus did a flourishing trade in images of the goddess and models of her shrine.[1]

It was they who came into conflict with St. Paul. At Ephesus he had found only a small group of Christians, who had experienced moreover only the incomplete baptism of St. John the Baptist. On his next visit he baptized them in the name also of the Holy Ghost, then launched on a long preaching campaign in the synagogue, until the Jews denounced him and he formed his own distinct Christian Church—the first of the Seven Churches of Asia. By two further years of patient reasoning and conversion, by a growing influence over Roman citizens, by miracles of healing, by the discrediting of the Jewish sorcerers and the public burning of their books, St. Paul and his Church obtained such a following, not only in Ephesus but beyond it, that the vested interests of the temple grew alarmed. During the month of the Artemision, when Ephesus was crowded with visitors, the silversmiths evidently found that their trade, thanks to St. Paul, was declining. Thus Demetrius, one of their master-craftsmen, called a meeting of his workmen and artisans, and incited them to a riot, which soon spread through the city. A mob swarmed down the broad marble streets and into the theatre, crying: 'Great is Diana of the Ephesians!' St. Paul hastened to follow and address them. But his disciples, and certain well-disposed Roman officials, dissuaded him, and the mob was finally appeased by an address from the Town Clerk.[2]

But St. Paul had broken the back of idolatry: the victory of Christianity was assured. The people of Ephesus came to worship the Panagia, the Virgin Mary, rather than Diana; and indeed, she would appear to them in visions, and perform miracles for them, much as the goddess had done. 'Great is the Panagia!' became the general cry.[3] No trace of the Temple of Artemis remains at Ephesus. It was looted by Nero and destroyed by the Goths, 'the rude savages of the Baltic . . .

[1] Authorities on the Temple of Artemis, quoted from Texier, Ximinez, Chandler, Broughton, and Barthélemy.

[2] Acts of the Apostles xix.

[3] Chandler, *op. cit.*

destitute of a taste for the elegant arts'.[1] Some of its columns found their way into the Church of St. Sophia at Constantinople; some of its sculptures are in the British Museum; the remainder of its stones may have well been taken by the Turks to build their mosque nearby. But there survives, in the opposite quarter of the city, a different place of worship: the shell of the great double church, the first to be dedicated to the Virgin, where the fifth-century councils of Ephesus were held. In the second century this was a Roman bank and exchange; in the fourth century it was converted into a Christian basilica. Plinths and columns still survive in its structure from the earlier classical building. But it has, as it were, been purged and purified. The lavishness of the Ephesian decoration, the pagan luxuriance of marble fruits and vines and scrolls have been swept away. Here, simple in design, austere in style, is an octagonal Christian baptistery. In the centre of its floor is a sunken marble basin, into which the candidates for baptism stepped. Covering its walls are panels of polished marble, severely plain but for a single sculpted symbol—the Cross. Here, surviving in stone, is the essence of the new civilization, the symbol of St. Paul and his victory.

A less happy symbol is the so-called burial place of the Virgin herself, to which the Turks, zealous to show their religious tolerance and abetted by the Roman Catholic community of Smyrna, now seek to attract a trade in pilgrims. There is a tradition, unsupported by historical evidence, that the Virgin, entrusted by Christ to St. John, came with him after the Crucifixion to Ephesus, where she lived out the rest of her days. It was here, runs the legend, and not at Jerusalem that she was buried, before her Assumption. But the site of her tomb remains unknown. In the nineteenth century a German nun, Catherine Emmerich, had a vision in which she saw precisely the place, on a mountain above Ephesus, where the Virgin had lived and died. Following her detailed directions, a series of French ecclesiastics searched for the spot, and eventually found a ruined house which coincided with her description. Moreover the local Christian villagers, whose ancestors had taken refuge in these mountains from the Islamic invasions, called the place Panagia Kapoulou, Our Lady of the Gate, and together with other orthodox pilgrims celebrated the feast of her Dormition here each year. Catherine Emmerich had stated that the Virgin's tomb was a mile-and-a-half from the house, near the last station of the Cross. It has yet to be found. But the local Catholics are

[1] Gibbon. *The Decline and Fall of the Roman Empire*, Chapter X.

satisfied, the Vatican has given a non-committal blessing, and the Turks have built an expensive tarmac road up to the holy place on the mountain.[1]

The place stands high, amid scrub which once was forest, at the head of a fertile valley, winding down to the sea. The house of the Virgin, which may date from as late as the fourteenth century, is a Byzantine chapel, once mellow with weathered stone and brick, now faced all over, as good as new with courses of smart white plaster, half smothering the mediaeval masonry. Inside, still less survives of the original wall surface; the floor is paved with a yellowish pseudo-mosaic, and concrete domes, incongruously oblong, have replaced the ruined cupolas. Outside, beneath a tree which grows out of the building, by a well now cleanly encased in concrete, are tables and chairs where the pilgrims may sit, writing post-cards and drinking bottled lemonade. There is a spacious car-park, and soon no doubt there will be a handsome hotel. By an image of the Virgin, in a prominent position, stands a substantial offertory-box. The shrine is unlikely to attract a tourist trade on the scale of the former Temple of Artemis. But at least it is in the Ephesus tradition.

The burial of St. John himself at Ephesus, after he had written the Apocalypse on the island of Patmos opposite, is more probable. The ruins of a cruciform church, built by Justinian on a hill to the east of the city, cover the vault where his tomb was said to lie. It contains columns whose acanthus capitals, forswearing the pagan, are stylized in the formal Byzantine manner. This was destroyed in its turn, and the Seljuk conquerors built a handsome mosque, which has preserved Ephesian continuity by the use of columns and stones from pagan temples and Christian churches alike. Chandler described it, unfairly, as a 'great though inelegant structure'. Severe as a barracks without, it has a walled courtyard, where an aged pistachio tree blooms by a fountain, and the jackdaws chip away, as though chiselling inscriptions in the stone. Within, broad rectangular windows frame the deep blue sky beyond. Its carpet today was of grass, smooth as a well-trimmed lawn, youthfully green in the shafts of sunlight which poured through its two broken domes. But the Turks were restoring their elegant brickwork, so that soon it would wither and die. When Arundell visited the mosque, he was shown an object protruding from the dome and assumed that it was an arrow, shot there by Tamurlane. Thereupon

[1] Rustem Duyuran. *Ephèse*. Ankara: 1951.

his companion, with a certain lack of tact, shot it down, and it was found to be a portion of chain, which had once carried a lamp.[1]

From the mosque in the evening I looked back across the plain, where the temple once stood, towards the hill, Mount Prion, which gave birth to it. The Ephesians lacked marble with which to build their temple. One day, however, a shepherd was feeding his flocks on the hill when a pair of rams began to fight. One, missing his antagonist, struck the rock with his horn, breaking off a crust of the whitest marble. He ran back with it to the city, where he was honoured and finally canonized for his discovery, being given the name of Evangelus, the Good Messenger.[2] Monthly sacrifices were still being made to him in the time of Augustus. Mount Prion today, with its friable limestone rock, is a necropolis of ancient tombs, carved out of it both by man and by nature: that of the Seven Sleepers, who slept through two centuries of Christian persecution and awoke when it was over; those of countless others who sleep there still; that, surely, of the Matron of Ephesus, whom Petronius immortalized. Inconsolable at the death of her husband, she spent days and nights in the vault, fasting and lamenting by his corpse. Here she was found by a sentry, guarding the corpses of some thieves who had been crucified nearby. After a few more days he succeeded in consoling her, first by meals and then by more intimate attentions. While he did so the parents of one of the thieves removed his body from the cross. Seeing that it was missing, the sentry was ready to kill himself rather than face punishment. But the widow protested: 'Heaven forbid that I should watch the bodies of the two dearest men in the world!', and insisted that he put her husband's corpse on the vacant cross in its place.[3] During the reign of Julian the Apostate, a sophist called Maximus used these caves for midnight orgies and Eleusinian mysteries, into which the Emperor was initiated.

In a strange blend of autumn and second spring the plain lay before me, patched with the warm brown of cotton and the cool green of fresh young pasture. The fig trees in their well-kept gardens, sources of sweet dried fruits for foreign markets, flamed leafy yellow or smoked leafless grey, between ranks of candle-like poplars. In the stillness of the evening the crying of children, the lowing of oxen, the braying of asses rang far and clear. Meanwhile, as night fell on the walls of the abandoned Byzantine citadel—to Chandler 'a large and barbarous

[1] Rev. F. V. J. Arundell. *A Visit to the Seven Churches of Asia*. London: 1828.

[2] Vitruvius, quoted by Chandler. *op. cit.*

[3] *Satyricon.*

edifice'—there came sounds of music and bursting rockets from the village of Selcuk,[1] beneath it. For the villagers were celebrating the Feast of Turkish Independence. The two cobbled streets had been decked with Turkish flags and garlands of box, and the bust of Atatürk on its marble plinth was wreathed, in appropriate homage. Around the arches of the towering Roman viaduct, throwing long weird shadows in the flaring light of swaying paraffin torches, the men danced to the irregular rhythm of drums and the monotonous lament of a pipe. It was a solemn dance, demanding tense concentration, like a disciplined drunken stagger. Each went through its motions in solitude, swiftly crouching, slowly rising, then balancing on tenterhooks, first on one leg, next on the other, for an eternal suspended moment. The women in their kerchiefs, so recently veils, looked on in silence, squatting by the piers of the aqueduct. The gendarmes kept order among the orderly crowd, stirred to action only when a genuine drunk swayed out of the wine-shop to join in the dance, and did it better than all the rest.

[1] Modern spelling of Seljuk.

CHAPTER II

PHRYGIA

Up the Valley—The Menderes Régime—A Scotsman in Aydin—A Cabaret in Denizli—The White Cliffs of Hierapolis—Latter-day Laodicea—An Unknown Civilization

FROM EPHESUS I travelled by train up the Meander valley into the Phrygian highlands. At the station of Selcuk the engine-driver took on two bottles of wine for himself and his mate—a pleasing gesture, showing a habit derived from the Greeks, since the Turks are not normally wine-drinkers. At each station shrill small boys in tweed caps hurried along the train selling food and drink—glasses of water and *ayran*, sour milk; sticky pastries, nuts and a tasteless fruit which otherwise resembled the strawberry; *köfte*, meat balls, wrapped in loaves of bread; *kebabs*, grilled with tomatoes and peppers on charcoal trays. Among the crowds there was an air of contentment, for the valley was booming. In Turkish it is the Menderes, from which the current Prime Minister, Adnan Menderes, took his name. Until Atatürk limited the big estates his family owned much of the land here. Anticipating the break-up, they sold off the surplus before the law was introduced, at a favourable price, and what remains to them, as a family, still returns a good profit.

Adnan Menderes was the strong man of Turkey—a strong man elected by the people, not imposed on them, like his predecessors, but perhaps growing too strong for a people who valued democracy. With a huge majority in Parliament, he was ruling the country in effect through a quadrumvirate, which he dominated, and which included also the President, Celal Bayar. It was a rule which was releasing the people from state control, and launching them on a career of free enterprise, lavishly backed by state finance. Its beneficiaries were peasants and landowners, whose productive effort, it was hoped, would convert Turkey, with American aid, into a prosperous exporting country. Here, among his own lands, the peasants were already profiting from a 'Menderes régime for the Menderes Valley'. The government had brought them new canalization, fertilizers to enrich new fields no longer flooded with silt, tractors to cultivate them, loans to develop them, usually in terms of cotton, subsidies for the prices of their crops. Mr. Menderes, himself a capitalist, was thus creating a new race of small peasant capitalists around him. In the evenings, driving their tractors, they bowled along the new roads, joy-riding with their families in trailers behind them. They had money to spend, whether on gold or refrigerators. They had not yet caught the habit of investment. But the banks, throughout the country, were doing their best to encourage it. In gay shop-windows, neon-lit and dressed by experts, they tempted the investor with lottery prizes—radio-sets, washing-machines, models of ideal homes. One bank, understanding peasant psychology, had offered, as first prize to its investors, a bag of gold.

At Aydin I found, unexpectedly, a Scotsman. He was there to make liquorice, an industry managed since the nineteenth century by the Scottish firm of Macandrew and Forbes. Some thirty years ago their business here was sold to an American firm. But Americans did not take to factory life in the lonely Meander valley, and Scotsmen continued to serve them in the field. They lived here contentedly, self-contained, two families in Aydin, two in Söke and one in Nazilli, relaxing in cosy cretonned English interiors, eating plain English food, drinking bottled English beer, reading the illustrated papers and listening to the football news on the radio. The liquorice root, uncultivable by man, is picked up wild from the fields where nature has planted it, in the wake of the plough or the harvester, by seasonal labour imported from the Phrygian plateau. A yellowish weed, it is then boiled in a factory and turned into a paste for export. My Scottish host was on good terms with the Turks, and took me to call on the Mayor of Aydin, a doctor who had abandoned his practice to serve the municipality. He was a conscientious man reluctant, as the oriental is, to delegate responsibility, hence working day and night. As he talked, the usual stream of callers passed in and out of the room: a woman, whom he fined for emptying slops outside her house; an ex-soldier, from Korea, applying for a driving-licence; a man wanting money to go to Muğla whom he sent out to be searched, suspecting that he had it already, concealed about his person, for a nefarious political purpose.

Beyond Aydin the valley meandered serenely upwards, bathed in a mellowing autumn light. The mountains, violet on one bank, blue on the other, swept down, no longer aloof but intimate in their demeanour, to fruitful fields and vineyards. The trunks of the fig trees flung shadows of indigo across the fertile wet red earth. The leaves of the pomegranates were yellowing, their fruit turning to gold; the vine-leaves were turning to purple. The planes were fading, their fine-cut leaves floating gently over the windless air. But the mulberries still spread boughs of green over a ploughland where cattle, unseasonably, grazed once more, finding gratuitous crops of thrusting young green shoots. Brighter and greener than the rest in this renewal of spring were the threshing-floors, neat round emerald carpets, laid for the peasants by the walls of their villages. Less ephemeral was the ripening autumn harvest, spread over the folds of the earth in a rich dark patchwork of maize and tobacco and cotton. Here bright-clad women picked industriously, loading the bales on to camels while boys on donkeys careered over the pastures, rounding up the cattle to bring them home. Weaving its way through the land, narrowing to a stream as it climbed, the Meander, stroked by the boughs of willows, gleamed blue in the evening sunlight.

Towards dusk we turned away from it up the valley of the Lycus, and came into Denizli, the market town which serves the upper Meander basin. I was conveyed to a hotel, where a Bulgarian boy, pale, fair and alert, took charge of myself and my baggage, showed me to an adequate room and enquired as to my needs with a zeal unfamiliar in his oriental kinsmen. He was one of the Moslem refugees, pushed into Turkey by the Communists from behind the Iron Curtain, who were being speedily settled in villages throughout Anatolia. He took me to a restaurant, where I dined and watched a cabaret entertainment. On the stage, advertising an American brand of radio, a life-size cardboard pin-up girl wooed her microphone in a sinuous enveloping embrace. Before her, in flesh and blood beneath a naked electric light bulb, five Turkish girls sat squarely in a row on upright chairs. Their plump squat forms, the Turkish Delight of today, were clothed in varying shades of pink and mauve and turquoise, with golden bracelets encircling their wrists, and perhaps an emerald-green cardigan flung over a shoulder to meet the chill of the evening. One, with an air of sophistication, wore dahlias in her hair and at other strategic points. At the tops of their voices, straight from the throat, they warbled a series of songs, unaccompanied and in unison, in the style of some voluptuous, profane *Muezzin*. The noise was cleverly magnified, to a prodigious extent, by a series of loudspeakers which often gave screams on their own. In the intervals the girls sat stolidly on their chairs, giggling a little at the audience, tweeded peasants in caps, drinking *raki* or beer, who gazed back at them with expressions of silent wonder. When she felt inclined, a girl would waddle off stage to change her dress, reappearing in a pattern of spirals; or another, upholstered in cretonne, with a flash of gold teeth, would stand square before the microphone, gripping it firmly with both hands lest it escape, crooning a sturdy solo, and at its climax removing her hands to flap them stiffly up and down against her thighs.

Denizli, thanks to cotton in particular and the Menderes régime in general, was clearly a prosperous peasant town. The music of the radio blared across the market place from half-a-dozen different shops, selling the latest American sets. Among its congested traffic, Land-Rovers were beginning to outnumber the painted peasant carts. The bazaar, shaded by vines, was festooned with coils of all sizes of ropes, and gaudy stuffs, while the sacks of grain were still embroidered in the traditional peasant style. For a few shillings I bought a coin of Nero and another of Alexander the Great. But the more popular shops were filled with pressure lamps, fancy glassware, chromium wristwatches and multi-coloured bicycles. For ever blundering their way through the crowds were buses bringing peasants, immured in their villages for centuries, to this fabulous centre of civilization.

But it was a different centre of civilization which I had come to see, the place which the Turks call Pamukkale, the Cotton Castle, and the Greeks and Romans called Hierapolis. From the train I had noticed its strange white cliffs—the 'cotton cliffs'—fringing the opposite slope of the valley. Now I took a car to visit the city, a watering-place of the Romans and of the Kings of Pergamum before them, which stands on a limestone tableland, jutting out from the mountains. Its ruins, dominated by a theatre and built from a porous golden stone, lie spread over a wide expanse of grassland, commanding a majestic prospect: the Meander plain, the valley of the Lycus, rising in Lycia, Mount Cadmus and the mountains of Caria. Their Roman baths and Byzantine basilicas, massive in scale and design, maintain an affinity of style so close that only a Cross, carved in the keystone of an arch, may distinguish profane from sacred. Covering the slope of a hill, beyond the walls, is a classical city of the dead. Its tombs and sarcophagi, one and all, have been rudely burst open and ruthlessly plundered, their doors and lids lying strewn over the ground as at some wholesale Resurrection. All is over at Hierapolis, even perhaps the Day of Judgment.

Somewhere, carved out of the face of its eroded mountain, is Charon's Cavern, the Plutonium. Strabo describes it as deep, but only wide enough to admit one man. A wide railing was built round the mouth of the cave, which exuded a cloud of dark and noxious vapour. 'Animals which enter within the railing', he recorded, 'die instantly. Even bulls, when brought within it, fall down and are taken out dead. We have ourselves thrown in sparrows, which immediately fell down lifeless. The Galli, who are eunuchs, enter the enclosure with impunity, approach even the opening or mouth, bend down over it, and descend into it to a certain depth, restraining their breath during the time, for we perceived by their countenance signs of some suffocating feeling.'[1] He confesses ignorance as to whether this immunity from the cave's ill-effects applied to all eunuchs, or only to those of the temple. The Plutonium is mentioned by several classical writers. But only one modern traveller claims to have seen it. This was Cockerell,[2] who 'found several small birds lying dead near the grotto; and though he tried its effects on a fowl for a whole day and without any result, he was assured by the inhabitants that it was sometimes fatal to their sheep and oxen, but that it was not always equally dangerous'. Chandler was told by a Turk that it was often fatal to goats, and that it was believed to be the home of a demon or evil spirit. But he had to leave Hierapolis before he could see it. Texier suggests that the cave was a narrow well which exuded a carbonic acid gas, heavier than air.

But it was the water, not the gas, which made a spa of Hierapolis. The phenomenon of the city is a deep clear pool, with grassy banks embellished by blushing oleanders. Its crystalline waters reveal depths of limpid blues and greens, from which stalactites and other such growths emerge with luminous clarity. The silver beads of a spring bubble swiftly to the surface, bursting in pins and needles of light to form a myriad minute eddies. The drums of fluted columns lie in the depths, still of the purest white, while others give form to the banks. Within a wooden enclosure a broken stair leads down into the pool, seeming to promise the bather a cool relief from the burning rays of

[1] *Geography*. Book XIII. The Galli were the Priests of Cybele.

[2] Quoted by Leake. *op. cit.*

the sun. Two brown boys were now splashing in it, diving from a fragment of Roman cornice. But the water around them was steaming gently. Dangling a foot in it, I found that it was hot, not cold.

Overflowing with exuberance, it runs this way and that, now as white as milk but still as clear as water, over the whitening earth and into a network of runnels, built up above it as though with concrete. But the steaming water itself has built them, transmuting everything into stone as it runs. The process, as of some cement factory managed by nature, is swift. Reeds and plants in its path turned, as I watched, to a glutinous substance which would soon petrify, fading in colour to a paler stonier green. In innumerable channels the water races over the cliffside, 300 ft. down, which it has been forming for centuries and still forms incessantly: a hot white stone cascade, streaked boldly with the browns and greens and yellows of the earth and the vegetation which it has engulfed and encrusted in its flow. Each channel and pool flings up walls, like layers of paralysed waves, above, below and before it, giving to the precipice, as they harden, a convex bone structure of giant concentric ribs and stylized limbs. The ancients ascribed this phenomenon to the action of the moon, visiting Endymion as he lay asleep by his herds and causing them to spill their milk around. The moderns ascribe it rather to the action of carbonic acid gas on calcium salts, which, as the gas evaporates, deposit themselves as an alkaline crust on all they touch. The water is so soft that it cleans the hands without soap. Apart from its medicinal virtues, the Romans found it useful for dyeing the rich wools of the neighbourhood, particularly in the purple; and indeed neighbouring waters dyed even the sheep which drank from them.

Today the villagers, living at the foot of the cliff, harness it to build walls and conduits for their cotton-fields, thus giving a new significance to the name Pamukkale. The verandahs of their houses look out on to the strange bleached steaming landscape, as on to an unfamiliar planet. In the coffee-shop an old man asked me the time, then showed me proudly a gold American watch, wearing it upside down on his wrist to admire the works, since the dial meant nothing to him. It was a far cry from this somnolent village to the Hierapolis of the ancients, to the spring festivals when multitudes thronged to the sanctuary of Astarte. 'While the flutes played, the drums beat, and the eunuch priests slashed themselves with knives, the religious excitement gradually spread like a wave among the crowd of onlookers, and many a one did that which he little thought to do when he came as a holiday spectator to the festival. For man after man, his veins throbbing with the music, his eyes fascinated by the sight of the streaming blood, flung his garments from him, leaped forth with a shout and seizing one of the swords which stood ready for the purpose, castrated himself on the spot. Then he ran through the city, holding the bloody pieces in his hand, till he threw them into one of the houses which he passed in his mad career. The household thus honoured had to furnish him with a suit of female attire and female ornaments, which he wore for the rest of his life. When the tumult of emotion had subsided, and the man had come to himself again, the irrevocable sacrifice must often have been followed by passionate sorrow and lifelong regret.'[1]

* * *

I drove back across the valley to the stony hillside, where Laodicea once stood. A city which thrived on the Roman clothing trade, and later a Christian see, it is today a desolate place—as indeed travellers have observed. Wheler described it as 'utterly destroyed and forsaken of man, an habitation only for Wolves, Foxes and Chacals, a Den of Dragons, Snakes and Vipers'. For did not the Lord warn the Laodiceans: 'Because thou art lukewarm, and neither hot or cold, I will spew thee out of my mouth?' [2] Hamilton wrote that 'nothing can exceed the desolation and melancholy appearance of the site', while Fellows found it deserted, but for a hundred eagles after the bones of a camel, and cutters of gravestones quarrying from the temple.

Since the destruction of the city no village has taken its place. But I did not find the site entirely deserted. A peasant was trying indefatigably to plough up Laodicea, with its massive ruined stadium, and there were traces of stubble where he had harvested a wheat crop. But it was hard ungrateful land, strewn in profusion with the rubble and sherds and blackening stones of the city. Mounds and terraces defied the plough, because of the buildings which still lay buried beneath them, and as he laboured the ploughman was for ever unearthing a Roman coin, a fragment of pottery, a boulder which proved to be the limb of a goddess—small consolation for the sparseness of his wheat crop. An amphitheatre of mountains framed the stony ploughland, their forms on the one hand stylized in a dark silhouette against a pale

[1] Sir James Frazer. *The Golden Bough*. London: 1922.

[2] Revelation iii, 16.

transparent sky, on the other still lit in their natural tones by the slowly declining sun. The eroded foothills, hard in their folds but soft in their shadows, fell around their flanks into the fertile plain, where the poplars of autumn stood guard over the crops of the Laodicean second spring.

* * *

The source of the Meander is at Dinar, a country town with painted houses and streets all gay with its waters. Here, having tunnelled its way from a lake, through a mountain, it bursts forth from the rock to start its sinuous career as a river. Close to these head-waters, where already the Meander has made a broad rich valley between the mountains, and where its marshes today are being canalized over the land and back into the main stream, is the village of Çivril whose mud-brick houses have spacious verandahs and fretted doors and cupboards. Near it, at Beyçesultan, by a crossing of the river on an ancient trade route, a city has been found, which is the centre of an unknown civilization. It contains a palace built late in the fifteen century B.C. and burnt down early in the fourteenth. It was a home of the Arzawa, a people who seem to have held the mountains and valleys of south-west Asia Minor, while the Hittites held the plateau, and to have rivalled the Hittites in military power, if not in cultural development. They were a people in diplomatic relations with Egypt, a people moreover in contact, probably hostile, with the Mycenaeans who held Miletus and with the Minoans of Crete. Beyçesultan is now being excavated by Mr. Seton Lloyd, Director of the British Institute of Archaeology at Ankara, who carries on the traditions established by a long line of British archaeologists in Turkey, and who has made valuable discoveries in a variety of fields. The city may well provide a missing link between the peoples of the Aegean, in the late Bronze Age, and the peoples of the Anatolian interior. Mr. Lloyd associates the Arzawa with the great Indo-European migrations of the second millennium B.C., which also populated Troy and perhaps even Greece. The Greeks could thus be of Anatolian, not Balkan origin. It is a tempting theory.[1]

[1] The excavations are described by Mr. Lloyd in *The Times* of June 10 and 24, July 6, September 23, 1954, and January 29 and November 26, 1955.

CHAPTER 12

LYDIA

The Hermus Valley—Sardis and its Temple—Manisa and its Mosques—The Weeping Goddess—Ayvalik—Pergamum and its Terraces—The Origins of Parchment—A Hellenistic Spa

THE HERMUS RIVER matches the Meander, running parallel and to the north of it from the highlands of Lydia, down into the Gulf of Izmir. Here, leaving the train at a wayside station, I walked a mile across the fields to the ruins of Sardis, lying at the foot of Mount Tmolus. A prosperous city from the days of Croesus until the days of St. Paul, a key point, commercial and strategic, on the Royal Road from the Aegean across Asia, it bore the weight like Laodicea of Apocalyptic censure: 'Thou hast a name that thou livest, and thou art dead . . . If therefore thou shalt not watch, I will come as a thief, and thou shalt not know what hour I will come upon thee.' [1] Wheler was not surprised to find Sardis 'a nest of worse than beggars'. Arundell asked, where were the churches of the Christians? 'The tumuli beyond the Hermus reply, "All Dead!", suffering the infliction of the threatened judgment of God, for abuse of their privileges. Let the unbeliever then be asked, is there no truth in prophecy, no reality in religion?'

Croesus drew his gold from the river of Sardis, the Pactolus, which ran through the market-place. The Romans, when the gold was worked out, took dye from its madder and wool from its sheep, weaving carpets as the Persians had done before them. Today the city, condemned by the Prophet, abandoned by man, has neither riches nor carpets. But the golden lights of the plateau still bathe its ruins, lying amid the rose-coloured folds of a soft eroded landscape. Above it, beyond a Byzantine acropolis, rise the slopes of Mount Tmolus, still dark with oak and pine. Beside it runs the Pactolus, its alluvial waters

[1] Revelation iii, 2.

still burnished as though with the gold dust, its boulders weathered and polished, dark as nuggets. Time moreover has gilded the two surviving columns of the temple of Cybele, the Mother Goddess of Lydia. Ionic and unfluted, they still stand serenely amid fallen drums and the blackened stones of an architrave, with a small Byzantine chapel sheltering beneath them. Three more columns, according to Cockerell, were thrown down by the Turks, 'For the sake of the gold which they expected to find in the joints'. The earlier temple was burnt during the Ionian revolt, together probably with all that remained of the capital of Croesus, and it was to avenge the temple's destruction that Darius invaded Attica to fight the battle of Marathon.

Sardis had fallen to the Persians, in the first place, largely because the horses of Croesus could not endure the unfamiliar sight or smell of the Persian camels. The Persians made gardens here and, according to Xenophon, the Great King Artaxerxes used to work in them with his own royal hands. There is indeed a flavour of the gardens of the Persian plateau in the golden planes, shading the banks of the river, and in the rose-pink soil threaded with yellowing vines and orchards. The practical Turkish peasants, having harvested their crop, were now busily damping the earth, mixing straw in it, and packing it, like mud-brick sheeting, into timbered frames on sound foundations of stone. In this manner they built themselves houses before the winter set in.

* * *

The train took me back to Manisa, a city where, for the first time in these classical lands, the traveller begins to sense the flavour of the Ottoman Empire. As Magnesia, it was a battlefield where the Romans defeated Antiochus the Great, driving him once and for all beyond the Taurus, and thus winning the Empire of the East. But it survives rather as Manisa, an alternative capital to Bursa and Adrianople of the early Ottoman sultans. It was to the soft caressing atmosphere of Manisa, warmed by the sunlight and cooled by the breezes of the lower Hermus valley, that Murad II, tiring of power and war, came in 1444 to live a life reconciling mystical reflection with sensuous ease and enjoyment. Surely the only sovereign in history voluntarily to abdicate and return to power twice over, he renounced the throne in favour of his second son, on the lamented death of his first. The son proving too young, at the age of fourteen, to deal with his Christian enemies, Murad returned to defeat them at the Battle of Varna, retired again to

Manisa, but returned once more to crush a revolt of the Janissaries, and died 'in harness', fighting the Hungarians.

Like the slopes of Mount Olympus at Bursa, the slopes of Mount Sipylus, here at Manisa, nourish gardens and orchards looking down over the broad abundant plain; and from among their trees rise the pencilled minarets, which describe the Ottoman skyline. Manisa is a miniature Bursa. The mosque built by the Seljuk conquerors is indeed massive enough, austere in style and incorporating the columns and other architectural relics of a large Byzantine church: for Manisa, during the Latin occupation of Constantinople, was for some twenty years capital of the Byzantine Empire. The Ottoman Turks finally secured the city after the departure of Tamurlane, who used it to store his accumulated spoils from Sardis and elsewhere. Their authority was disturbed only in the fifteenth century by the rebellion of a left-wing dervish fanatic, Bedz-ed-Din, who preached the doctrine of Poverty, Equality, and Common Ownership of property, and was defeated by Murad at the age of twelve—his first military victory. Hardly a trace remains of Murad's palace, whose gardens rivalled those of Bursa, or of the tombs where his family were buried. The main buildings which survive at Manisa are the work of the sixteenth-century Sultan Murad III—two mosques, a *medresse*, a domed building transformed into a museum. They lack the scale of the mosques at Bursa but, with their coloured tiles and delicate brickwork and fretted stained-glass windows, they achieve a similar refinement of style. As I walked among them, in the afternoon sunlight, the planes shed golden leaves into courtyards all bright with the autumn crocus. Materially Manisa afforded little to the traveller. The inn was clean, but its bedrooms had doors of glass, admitting a flood of light from the landing. I searched in vain for a restaurant, and finally found consolation in a wine shop, where the Turks of Manisa were drinking away like Greeks.

Next morning I walked for a mile or so along the road to the north of the city, beneath the slopes of Mount Sipylus. Here I expected to find Niobe, in stone. For this was the mountain whence Tantalus, displeasing the gods, was flung down to his death and eternal torment, thirsting for ever in a lake whose waters receded when he tried to drink them. It is a legend inspired or at least enhanced by the earthquakes which afflicted the region, engulfing the Lydian city of Sipylus where Tantalus reigned, and turning its marshes into lakes. One of them, as Strabo remarks, destroyed Magnesia in the reign of Tiberius.[1] Niobe, the daughter of Tantalus, met with similar misfortunes, being turned to stone on Mount Sipylus, after the massacre of all her children by the gods, her effigy continuing, in season, to shed tears. 'And now', wrote Homer, 'she stands among the crags in the untrodden hills of Sipylus, where people say the Nymphs, when they have been dancing on the banks of Achelous, lay themselves down to sleep. There Niobe, in marble, broods on the desolation that the gods dealt out to her.'[2]

Presently I came to a lake, once doubtless a marsh, such as engulfed the city, now tidily harnessed to serve as a reservoir. Above it, looking down on the road from a cliffside, the weeping woman sits. Originally she was thought to be an illusion, a freak of nature. Pausanias 'saw only the rock and precipice; nothing whatever which resembled a woman, either weeping, or in any other posture; but if you stood at a distance, you would fancy that you beheld a woman in an attitude of grief, and in tears'.[3] Chandler describes her as 'an effect of a certain portion of light and shade on a certain part of Sipylos, perceivable at a particular point of view'. Neither can have scaled the cliffside. Chishull, doing so in the eighteenth century, describes her accurately;[4] Arundell states that 'Mr. McFarlane was more adventurous than Dr. Chishull, and measured the lady's figure'. Van Lennep's Greek guide told him: 'There is a tradition that this statue was once a woman, and her children were killed, and she wept so that God changed her to stone. They say her tears make a pond down there, and still keep it full.' He added that, while the English were building the railway, they stood at the outer rock, and fired with ball at the face of the statue. 'More likely', comments Van Lennep, 'they were Turks.'[5]

'Niobe' is in fact Cybele, the Mother Goddess of Asia Minor, sculpted in bas-relief in a niche in the cliff-side by the Hittites. For more than two thousand years, the wind and the rain and the sun have worn away at her limestone limbs and features, restoring her, in aspect, to the source from which she came: a goddess fashioned not by man but by nature, an organic, living element in the womb of the rock. Stylized in form, colossal in scale, she sits, with hunched head and shoulders and abundant loins, brooding eternally down over the flanks

[1] *Geography*. Book XIII. [2] *Iliad*. Book XXIV. (Penguin translation.)

[3] *Description of Greece*. Book I.

[4] Rev. Edward Chishull. *Travels in Turkey*. London: 1747.

[5] H. J. Van Lennep. *Travels in Little-known Parts of Asia Minor*. London: 1870.

of the mountain to the plain and the lake, spread at its feet. Van Lennep, who knew nothing of the Hittites, draws an analogy between the children of Niobe, 'struck down to Earth, slain by Phoebus and Diana' and the rocks which the action of the elements has detached from the cliffside, strewing them over the ground beneath it. 'Tears' do in any case pour down the face and the robes of the statue: two streams of moisture, seeping down after the rain from the rock of Tantalus, poised above it, and disfiguring the golden stone with long black streaks.

* * *

The last of the great Aegean cities is Pergamum—the Bergama of the Turks. I came to it first from the North, leaving the mail-boat at Ayvalik, where the sombre narrows of the Dardanelles open out into the radiant expanse of a southern sea. Bounded on the horizon by the sun-baked shores of the island of Lesbos, approached by a channel no wider than an arterial road, Ayvalik is a natural harbour, its green seas locked by tawny islands and ochre sands. A mediaeval castle, posted on a headland, protects it. A ruined monastery on an island, a church on another, proclaim it a port till lately Greek, and there is a clean Greek air about its cobbled streets and colour-washed houses.

The café where I awaited the bus was bright with trappings of copper and brass, and the gear of the pipes, arrayed in rows on the shelves, was neatly coiled and polished. Faded photographs of Greek actresses in the fashions of the nineties, perching vases on their shoulders, flanked the sterner effigy of Atatürk in full evening dress. Gas lamps, with petals of frosted glass, shone down on an opulent nineteenth-century clock; on a white carved washstand, its taps adorned with a brass star and crescent; on an elaborate gilt mirror, crowned by a mythical winged beast, which bent over as though seeking its reflection in the glass. The Greek taste of the period had penetrated even to the mosque, whose columns and prayer-niche were painted in elegant marble *trompe l'œil*. Greek vigour, moreover, seemed to animate the Turks who sat around me. There was a babble of voices and a sharper rhythm in the slap of the *tric-trac* men on the board. One of the players, commercially-minded, offered me an English sovereign for the price of forty-five Turkish pounds.[1] Negotiations were interrupted

[1] About £5 10*s*.

by the arrival of my bus, which took me inland over the blue hills to Bergama.

* * *

Pergamum was not merely a city but a kingdom. Its dynasty was founded by a eunuch, Philetaerus. Alexander's general, Lysimachus, had used it as a fortress in which to hoard the spoils of his wars against the Persians, leaving the trusted Philetaerus to guard them. But his wife offended the eunuch, who turned against him, seized the spoils, and reigned on the proceeds for twenty years as an independent prince, in peaceful alliance with his neighbours. At his death the principality passed to his nephew, whose cousin and successor, Attalus, proclaimed himself King after a resounding victory against the Galatians. The Attalids held and expanded their kingdom through an astute policy of alliances with the Romans, to whom after 150 years they finally bequeathed it. They rivalled in power the Seleucids and Ptolemies, and their city won renown as a centre of art and culture. Ptolemy, jealous of its library as a rival to that of Alexandria, prohibited the export of papyrus from Egypt. So Pergamum evolved instead a superior form of parchment (*pergamentum*) from the skins of its herds, thus becoming, as Dallaway remarks, a place 'where literature was preserved, by writing, from the uncertainty and fluctuation of oral tradition'. Parchment was eventually recognized by Rome, in preference to papyrus, as being more easily produced, more durable, and 'more likely to assure the immortality of the texts'.[1] But the Ptolemies won in the end. The library of Pergamum—or at least two hundred thousand of its volumes—was given by Antony to Cleopatra when one of the libraries of Alexandria was burnt.

Pergamum is a city built on a mountain, a towering crag, between two streams which served the city, in its early days, for defence. But it is a classicized crag. The Greeks who created Pergamum scorned to build vertically, following the irregular contours of their slope, as a Romantic or a mediaeval age might have done. Instead, with infinite skill and labour, they built horizontally, taming and flattening the rock to impose upon it a classical sequence of ordered courts and terraces. Pergamum is a mountain transformed into a monument. Layer above layer it rises, converting slopes into stairways, crags into buttresses, cliffs into walls, contriving at each stage to create a prospect of paved, level spaces and buildings of ample scale.

[1] Ximinez. *op. cit.*

At the foot of the rock stand the towering ruins of an immense basilica with two rotundas, traditionally a Christian church, but evidently a Roman place of worship, or perhaps Roman baths before it. Above it, along the first of the city's four great terraces, stretches the *agora*, with relics of pavement and of shops behind a severe, rectangular Doric colonnade. Inscriptions have survived here, regulations as to policing of the streets, the upkeep of buildings, the control of exchange and commerce.

Today humanity survives only in fragments of marble, strewn haphazard over the site. Amid the drums of columns lie the broken limbs of statues, a pile of hands and feet, a stout pair of buttocks, a single toe in a sandal, a hand holding the tassels of a robe. From the market four roads, meeting in a crescent, lead steeply to different parts of the town. The main street mounts in a stately curve, paved with broad slabs of stone, flanked by a massive Greek wall, to a rounded gateway and the remains of a fountain, some eighty feet long, where water once gushed from a procession of taps for the refreshment of the city and its people. Through the gateway a long covered stairway, with a smooth and mortarless barrel-vault, leads upwards, an architectural rarity, perhaps inspired by the East, since the Greeks in the second century did not normally vault their buildings.[1]

It emerges on to a terrace like a great university campus, the site, at three different levels, of three gymnasia, as it were primary, secondary and undergraduate. Their rooms give on to long arcades, Doric in Greek times, Corinthian in Roman, forming three sides of the spacious quadrangle. There is an Odeon, like a small Sheldonian Theatre. There are Roman baths on an ostentatious scale with various gradations of rooms, from cool to hot, a furnace-room to heat them and an elaborate system of plumbing. There is a Greek bath, simpler and more austere, built in a style reminiscent of a Byzantine church, its washroom furnished with rows of marble basins. There are rooms where the youths stripped and oiled for their sports and, stretching under cover beneath them, a racetrack more than two hundred yards long. There is a wall where, in schoolboy fashion, the pupils have scratched their names.

The upper terrace of the mountain city is devoted to its temples. Two smooth columns, with lotus capitals, lead the way into a long avenue, terraced out of the cliff side and lined with tiers of seats. At the

[1] Sartiaux. *op. cit.*

end a small portico of fluted columns enshrines the altar of Demeter, who presided here, in the shadow of the mountain, over Eleusinian mysteries. Here too, around the summit, lie the marble stones—the cornices and capitals, the scrolls and garlands—of shrines where Dionysus and Athena, Caracalla and Trajan were honoured. Crowning all, in the centre of a great colonnaded platform, stood the altar of Zeus from whose monumental ruins a single pine-tree grows. No contemporary writer has described it, though Pausanias mentions, at Olympia, 'an altar of Zeus resembling that which exists at Pergamum'.[1] But it was unearthed in the nineteenth century by German archaeologists, a vast Ionic structure, or complex of structures, whose exuberant mythological friezes—now in Berlin—rank among the wonders of the Hellenistic world.

A library building survives at Pergamum, perched high on the rock, giving out on to a terrace where readers could take the air. A house survives, the home of Attalus, a rich patrician, handy in size and elegant in taste. Its rooms, with cellars and baths beneath them, open on to a courtyard, embellished with busts and fountains and enjoying a fine view of the valley beneath. Their floors are paved with bright mosaic, their walls painted with murals, Pompeian in style, with sprays of flowers suggesting the later tulip designs of the Turks. Inscriptions record the good fare and good wine dispensed by the host, and his respect for the goddess Cybele. But the outstanding architectural achievement of Pergamum is the theatre. The stage is built out from a precipitous slope on an artificial terrace, reinforced with buttresses, a shallow semi-circle, with an abrupt drop down to the valley behind it. In the floor of the built-up Roman proscenium holes survive at regular intervals, made to hold the portable wooden structure which served the early Greeks as a scene. Before it the auditorium rises, sheer as a scree, up the face of the mountain, eighty steep rows of seats, stepped up to a height above the stage of a hundred and thirty feet.

From here I looked out over a lonely landscape of tired tawny hills, awaiting the relief of the first rains of winter. Right beneath me the two streams of Pergamum met, then wound on together in a dull gleam of silver, through the russet-roofed, blue-washed city of Bergama, and across a desiccated plain towards the sea. I climbed down and across to the 'spa' of Aesculapius, where the river's curative waters

[1] *Description of Greece*. Book VI.

attracted a large assembly of classical invalids. It was a Pergamum-les-Bains, where they bathed and sun-bathed, listened to music, had their dreams interpreted, received drugs and submitted to surgical operations at the hands of the priests. Here is the temple of the God of Medicine, with a row of slender Ionic columns, a small theatre, lately restored by the Turks, and a number of underground offices, built for the convenience of visitors. One of these is a well-built Hellenistic privy.

CHAPTER 13

TROAS

Stranded at Gallipoli—Across to Çanakkale—The Missing Wallet—The Plains of Troy—Where All Winds Meet—On the Banks of the Scamander—Achilles and the Anzacs—To Istanbul

THE CITY OF TROY stands at the head of the Aegean, within the shadow of the Dardanelles. Close to Chanak, now Çanakkale, it commands a vital area of naval defence, and is thus a hard place to visit. No foreigner, without permission from the Turkish Cabinet, may approach Çanakkale from inland; all must come by sea, moreover armed with permits for the Troad from the naval authorities. My first attempt to reach Troy was a failure. On arrival at Çanakkale from Istanbul I was informed that my permit covered only the town itself, not the surrounding country where the ruined city stands. So I continued on my journey. A month or so later I made a second attempt, this time, I hoped, with the necessary authority behind me.

All day long we pitched uncomfortably across a grey Sea of Marmara. After dark we reached the shelter of the Straits, drawing into Gelibolu, once Gallipoli, where a castle loomed over a miniature harbour, closely packed with fishing-boats. My boat drew alongside a modern quay beyond it. Learning that she was to stay here for an hour, I went ashore, to stretch my legs in the village. It offered me little, and after a stroll and a cup of coffee, I returned to the quay. It seemed strangely bleak and deserted and it was a moment before I realized why. The boat had gone, half-an-hour before her time. Bewildered, I returned to the coffee-shop wondering what to do next. All my belongings had gone with the boat, including a wallet, too fat for the pocket, containing passport, money, and, more vital, all the notes of a four months' journey.

An English-speaking Turk, in some kind of uniform, came to my rescue. He was, he explained, the interpreter to a group of American officers, attached to the Navy nearby. He took me to the police who looked solemn. They explained that I had no right to be here, in the closed naval area of Gelibolu, and requested me, politely but urgently, to leave. Very well; but how was I to do so? No boat was due, from either direction, for another three days. I could not proceed by land, since the western shores of the Gelibolu peninsula were strictly barred to foreigners. To hire a motor-boat, to take me across, would cost money, and I had none. Meanwhile, I suggested that an attempt should be made to put my baggage ashore, at Çanakkale, where the boat would soon be arriving. The police became busy. They sent a telegram to Çanakkale. They finally got through on the telephone, and with much shouting, which seemed to be inaudible in Çanakkale, left some instructions. Then a police sergeant conducted me, under police arrest, to an airless room, containing three hard beds, at an inn. Please, were his words, would I leave in the morning? I would do my best.

He awoke me in the morning. Please, he repeated solemnly, would I now leave? I had no permission to be here. Willingly, I replied, but how? He looked nonplussed. Then he went off to telephone once more to Çanakkale. This time a message came back from the *Vali* in person. I was authorized to proceed by bus, through the forbidden area on the European side of the Straits, to Eceabat, whence the ferry would take me across to Çanakkale. Meanwhile my baggage had been removed from the boat and was safely in his hands. Tension relaxed. The police sergeant went so far as to smile, and we drank coffee together. The interpreter took me to call on an American officer, who treated me to a can of beer, and invited me with a hint of nostalgia in his voice to visit him in South Carolina.

The bus bore me away into the prohibited area along the European shore of the Straits. I kept my eyes open, but saw nothing I should not see, only an undulating landscape of moorland and plough, beneath frowning wooded hills. The force of the prevailing sea-winds smoothed and rounded the brushwood as water rounds a stone; the trees leant away from it, their branches recoiling into patterns of a tortured symmetry. The Straits eddied restlessly beneath sullen grey clouds which suddenly parted, releasing a sunbeam to illuminate the waves with a malignant gleam. We were approaching the narrows, between Sestos and Abydos, marked by a Turkish castle on either side. The landscape opposite was so similar that the Hellespont seemed merely an accidental fissure in the land, and it was hard to see it as the gulf between two continents. It was the site nevertheless of historic crossings: where Xerxes built his bridge of 674 rafts, to invade Greece; where the Ottoman Turks first planted the crescent in Europe; where the army of Alexander first set foot in Asia. Leander had swum across here many times, to meet Hero, until 'wave is driven on wave, the sea is mounting high; the waves seem to mingle with the clouds; the winds roar from every quarter'[1]—and he was swept up lifeless at her feet, to be joined by her in death. Lord Byron, emulating him, swam across in sixty-five minutes, but found no Hero awaiting him. Held up for some weeks on his voyage from Smyrna to Constantinople, he lived at Abydos in a house beneath an immemorial elm, both of which still survive. The Turks point out the place to foreigners, expressing regrets only that the bad lord was no Moslem—then he would have been better.

At the ferry I was greeted in English by a Cypriot shopkeeper. He had come over to Gallipoli with a mule unit from Cyprus, during the First World War, and had stayed on after it. He showed me on to the boat, which bounced me across the waves to Çanakkale, a port with a clean and windswept Nordic air. A police officer received me and took me at once to the station, where my belongings, retrieved from the boat, were carefully laid out and listed for my identification. But the wallet, with all that I valued, was missing. I expressed concern, which was echoed by the police officer. Then I remembered that, when I left the boat, I had as a precaution swept a curtain over the wallet on the seat where it lay: it might thus have escaped notice. The Chief of Police reassured me, telephoned at once to the *Vali*, then put an urgent call for him through to the *Vali* of Izmir, where the boat should at that moment be arriving. Resigning myself to some further hours, if not days of anxiety, I proceeded to the house of an Englishman, the curator of the Gallipoli war cemeteries, who lived in Çanakkale and had invited me to stay. Imagining the almost impossible burden of writing a book about Turkey without notes, I found it hard to concentrate on his amiable conversation. But within half-an-hour there was a rap at the door. A police sergeant was outside. He saluted, and informed me that my wallet, with all it contained, was in the hands of the police at Izmir. Would I kindly advise the *Vali* what should be done with it? Not for nothing had I sensed a Nordic atmosphere,

[1] Apollodorus, quoted by Ximinez. *op. cit.*

as I tossed across the Hellespont. I blessed amenities rare in the Mediterranean, an honest ship's crew, an efficient police force, helpful officialdom, a telephone service which worked. Thenceforward Atatürk's stern portrait, in the government offices, took on a new and more personal significance.

The people of Çanakkale, my host assured me, were especially honest. At this season there was some thieving of warm clothes, as a precaution against the winter climate. Otherwise crime was rare. A prison sentence was unpopular in the family, since the prisoner had to be supplied with food from home. The honesty of the ship's crews was nevertheless remarkable, since they were poorly paid and lived largely on their tips. The police were concerned largely with the search for spies. Only a few days ago they had rounded up seven Bulgarians, caught without passports. My host had a large house on the front, solid with English comfort. But since his wife was in England, we ate our meals in a local restaurant, enjoying the excellent fresh fish of the Straits, in which the Greeks still traded, their caiques coming freely into the harbour to load. Relations between Greek and Turk were better here than in the South. The Jews also were respected, fulfilling their functions in the community as tailors, and earning a reputation for good manners. They had amassed gold in the past, selling lengths of cloth for necklaces. Now, for some reason, they preferred banknotes. When Dallaway went there the British Consul was a Jew, with a 'truly patriarchal house' containing 'four married couples with five generations under the same roof, through whom the same countenance is transmitted with striking resemblance, especially by females'.

My host was an excellent companion, popular with the Turks, well-informed as to their lives and customs. Together we drank the excellent wine from Tenedos, the island just off the Straits, which still has a Turco-Greek population: a dry vintage for my taste, a sweet one, resembling Madeira, for that of the Turks, who drank it to keep warm in the winter. They drank moderately. My host quoted one of their adages: 'One glass makes a sheep, two glasses make a lion, three glasses make a monkey.' As we ate he quoted another about the onion: 'For breakfast, eat it yourself; for lunch, give it to a friend; for dinner, give it to an enemy.' More macabre were tales of his experiences, collecting bodies for burial after the First World War, along the line of the Baghdad Railway. They were war prisoners from Kut who had died on the journey, their bones still lying, ten years later, in the tunnels where their corpses had been dumped from the trains.

Next morning we hired a car to drive, in the company of a policeman, to Çiplak, the Naked Village, where Troy once was. The road wound upwards through dust-gold oak trees, scattered tidily over the dark red ploughland. Their acorns enrich the people of the Troad who sell them for the manufacture of ink. We reached the top of a rise and there, spread beneath us, was the deep-soiled land of Troy. 'I could scarcely control my emotion', wrote Schliemann, 'when I saw the tremendous plain of Troy spread out before me, a scene that had haunted my earliest childhood dreams.'[1] With the flair and intuition of the amateur, he immediately placed the site of Troy here on the mound of Hissarlik, and not, as his predecessors had believed, on the mound of Bunarbaşi, some way inland. With watch in hand he paced the plain, backwards and forwards, between the mounds and the sea, re-fighting the battle from the pages of Homer. Then he began excavations which proved him right. Layer beneath layer, nine successive cities of Troy emerged, and among them he identified, as he thought, the Great Tower, the Scaean Gate, the palace of Priam, the high city walls of the Iliad. He was a thousand years or so out; this was an older city. But Priam's was there above it. The Troy of Homer was proved no legend.

Today the ground is strewn on the surface with the relics of Roman Troy: the elegant masonry, nicely inscribed, of a theatre and baths, drawing their water by pipes from Mount Ida. The older and more primitive cities have no such elegance. Re-creation of Troy from the warren of mounds and foundations and tunnels, which it has now become, demands the eye and the faith of the archaeologist. But here, outliving its ruins, is all its atmosphere. Here, unmistakably, are the steep streets of Ilium, the rough but well-built walls from which the Trojans looked down on the ebb and flow of battle. Closely confined by the rock on which it sits, it is a smaller, narrower city than Homer, who knew only a later Troy, described and perhaps imagined: in modern terms it is indeed hardly more than a village, its towers and walls and high, congested houses piled up above the plain like some mountain village of Italy or Greece today. Schliemann calculates that it can have held only five thousand inhabitants, with an army of five hundred soldiers.[2]

[1] C. W. Ceram. *Gods Graves and Scholars*. London: 1952.

[2] Dr. H. Schliemann. *Troy and its Remains*. London: 1875.

Troy 'of the broad streets' may be smaller in fact than in legend; but it is set in the very landscape which Homer portrayed. Here is the wide sweep of the battlefield, with its back to the ocean and to the swift-flowing Hellespont, facing layers of hills which rise up in perspective to the snow-covered peak of Mount Ida. Well-named by Homer windy Ilium, it is a corner of the world where all winds seem to meet, where the sea is constantly 'darkened by a soundless swell', waiting, like Nestor in his indecision, 'to begin its march till the wind sets in steadily from one side or the other'. The Iliad is indeed an epic of these winds and seas, with which the mariners of history—Achilles with his black ships, the Anzacs with their landing-craft—have battled to their cost. The north wind, following the current at the mouth of the Hellespont, stirs the swell, the south wind battles against it so that 'the great waves hiss and arch their foaming backs in a never-ending procession'.[1]

Today the calm glow of autumn fell on Troy, shedding purple lights over the deep brown soil and its splashes of young green pasture. The Hellespont lay still, shining a luminous blue; the island cones of Imbros and Samothrace stood up with transparent clarity from the seas beyond it. Seeking the Scamander and the Simois I walked down over the plain, towards the ridge which broke the west wind's force, and the sands in the lee of it where the Achaeans must have beached their ships. The Simois has vanished, drained away over the earth in pipes and channels, to give its waste-lands and marshes a fertility unknown to the Trojans. But the Scamander survives, forsaking its bed beneath the walls of the city to run through the heart of the plain, spreading canals to right and left of it. With the growth of cultivation, the thickets of tamarisk have gone from the plain, together with the elms and the willows and the wild fig tree of Homer. But there are rushes still by the grassy banks of the river, where I sat for a while in the stillness, as Ares and Athene did when she led him away from the battle. An eagle hovered silently above me; but there was no ominous, blood-red snake in his talons. Crossed by a long stone footbridge with a Turkish hump, the Scamander today is a gentle, sluggish stream, its silver eddies now dark with the mud of Mount Ida, but swirling and foaming with cataracts no longer.

Hector, issuing his challenge on the field of Troy, foretold the day when 'some future traveller, sailing by in his good ship across the wine-dark sea, will say: "This is the monument of some warrior of an earlier

[1] Quotations are from the Penguin translation of the *Iliad*.

day who was killed in single combat by illustrious Hector."' Today a monument does indeed command the Straits, from a height of a hundred and twenty feet. But it stands on the coast not of Troy but of Thrace, and recalls other battles, those of the First World War. It is the Helles memorial to twenty thousand soldiers, missing in the Gallipoli campaigns. My host, who was in charge of the war cemeteries, took me across to them in his motor-boat next day. Even for such an expedition he had to apply for a permit, several days in advance. The coast of Thrace stretched ahead of us, worn yellow and green like a faded length of sun-gilt tapestry. A Genoese castle crouched low on the water, heart-shaped and pierced by a rectangular tower as in some abstract modern design. The grass had grown over the old Turkish batteries, as on a cluster of abandoned tombs; the modern defences of the Straits were invisible.

The winds allowed us to land at V. Beach, opposite the beach of Achilles, by the wreck of a landing-craft, a rusty memorial as eternal as the monument which rose from the cliff-top. A cross on a pedestal, built not of marble from the Marmara, like the monuments of the Greeks, but of a dull grey stone from the Pennines, it had a strangely muted Nordic look beneath the glowing Aegean light. Italian masons had helped to build it, discouraged by a journey from Italy without wine in a British warship, chiselling the stone nevertheless with graceful Roman lettering. But the men who lie here, deep in 'rich-soiled Thrace', their bones nourishing vigorous waves of grass, are a race from the North, foreign to Achaeans, Trojans and Turks alike. They lie in gardens of myrtle and juniper, rosemary and cypress, the plants of the South, but beneath the headstones of their country, austerely carved and lettered. Sailors, soldiers, mariners and merchant seamen of the British Empire: 'Their glory shall not be blotted out . . . their name liveth for evermore'. But the salt of the Aegean is eating its way into the stone of the North, erasing the outlandish names. A few hundred years hence as little may remain, outside the pages of literature, of the heroes of Gallipoli as of the heroes of Troy.

* * *

Before my departure from Çanakkale in the middle of the afternoon, the *Vali* entertained me to a party at his house. A sophisticated *Vali*, with a westernized wife for hostess, he provided cocktails with snacks, followed by whisky-and-soda. He held the Istanbul boat back for an hour, from four to five, that we might continue to drink—rather to my disquiet, as I had to catch a train, within a narrow margin of time, next morning, and there was a heavy sea running in the Marmara. The boat moreover was small. But she rode the waves without effort and made up for lost time. She was the mail-boat from Imbros, the Greek island which the Turks took over with Tenedos, for the defence of the Straits, after the First World War. I talked with one of its islanders, a Greek storekeeper who knew English but had not spoken it for more than thirty years. During the First World War he had run a canteen on Cape Helles for the troops, so profitably, it seemed, that a certain British General had prophesied for him a millionaire's future. Only the accident of becoming Turkish had prevented the fulfilment of the prophecy—or so he implied. All the inhabitants of Imbros were Greek. They seldom learnt Turkish, obliging the Turks to learn Greek, and wished to revert to Greece. But they had no contact with the motherland, or even with the neighbouring Greek island of Samothrace. As an island, none the less, Imbros was self-supporting, importing only groceries, exporting its olive oil, its honey, its sponges—all but its wine, which the inhabitants preferred to drink.

We put in at Sarköy, on the Thracian coast: a wintry port in a landscape purpling as though with the increasing cold. Early in the morning a long serrated ridge lay ahead of us. As we drew closer the light transformed it slowly into a ridge of domes and minarets: the architectural skyline of Istanbul. Meeting the swift race of the Bosporus we rounded Seraglio Point, and drew into the Golden Horn.

CHAPTER 14

BYZANTIUM (I)

Istanbul—The Rhythm of Two Seas—Life on the Bosporus—The Islands of the Princes—Survivors from the Past—The Palaces of the Sultans—'Monsieur Rococo'

ISTANBUL is a classic example, unusual among cities, of a happy marriage—between nature and man. Land and water are its elements: the land resolved into architecture, the water forever girding away at it, the two coalescing to create a city instinct with space and speed and a liquid cleansing light. Its rhythm is in the water, in the Bosporus, racing like a deep salt river between Europe and Asia, from a cold sea in the North to a warm sea in the South. Restless with waves which can never break, it thrusts from one side to the other, stretching arms around headlands, lapping at mosques and palaces, with now a gentle, now a boisterous attention. All Istanbul is built on the sea. It is a city of windows, craning one above the other for a view of it and a smell of it and a reflection of its light, their panes glinting gold as the sun dies away from it into the green hills of Europe beyond.

Always I have stayed on the Bosporus, first in a long nineteenth-century palace, its bay-windows overhanging the water like those of some substantial seaside hotel; later in a large decaying wooden house in an overgrown garden beyond it. In the palace we would dine on the balcony and sit far into the night, wrapped warmly in darkness, at once stirred and lulled by the merged constellations of lights on the water and stars in the sky. Here, released from its narrows, below the pair of turreted watchdog castles once built to defend it from either shore, the Bosporus runs broad as a series of lakes. Every minute it is lit by a searchlight, from a penny steamer, sweeping the dark waves like a moonbeam from one shore to another, or by the white lamps of a fishing-fleet, strung low along the water, chugging northwards into the Black Sea night.

From daybreak the hurrying waters are alive with a galaxy of boats, painted within and without. Barges of all colours, with patched billowing sails, lumber across the current up wind. Ivory-white launches cut through the surface like swordfishes. Rowing boats, bright as kingfishers, hover over it, perhaps fishing, perhaps hawking pedlar's wares, or prawns, or corn-on-the-cob. Ocean liners, sometimes from Russia, ride the fairway with a majestic assurance. The penny steamers, punctual to the minute, speed as swiftly as trams from one pier to another, then impatiently on to the next. Faster than all of them, skimming low over the waves, fly the convoys of shearwaters, strong on the wing. Breeding on the Black Sea, feeding in the Marmara, they sit on the nest in shifts, male and female; but at the moment of hatching both parents desert it, leaving the young to fend for themselves.

Each morning I would bathe from the steps of the palace in cool deep waters, vigorous as champagne, contrasting sharply with the lukewarm Marmara shallows. Beyond me the village hugged its harbour, a crescent of unsubstantial painted houses, each with its verandah and its landing-stage and its boat moored beneath it—one of the villages strung out, in an unbroken procession, from one end of the sea to the other. Here is land- and sea-scape clean as in an aquatint, drained of perspective by the glassy, almost Nordic light. Rows of gentlemanly houses, built from weathering timber and enamelled with plaster in various colours, lie flat along the water, against green hills tangled with woods and neglected rambling gardens. At their windows, on their balconies, in their gardens of trim bright flower-beds, bourgeois life is lived openly before all who sail by. Family groups sit stolidly, gazing for ever at the water, waving politely at the steamers, eating meals, reading newspapers, playing with children, teasing cats. A man fishes in his pyjamas. Boys bathe in their pants. Pigeons flutter on the roof-tops. Gulls wheel around the ships. Cafés and restaurants on stilts bulge out over the water, overflowing with crowds from the city.

The Istanbulis are a people who love a view and a picnic, by the water's edge or in the woods inland. Here the oaks and the beeches of the forest of Belgrad shade reservoirs, aqueducts and marble dams, built by emperors and sultans to water the city: and here families come on Sundays, to cook and eat their own food, to swing in hammocks or in swings, dance to the gramophone, amuse the children with Blind Man's Buff among the samovars. Picnickers squat on grassy banks, by the Sweet Waters of Asia, rambling amid gardens and hedgerows like some backwater of the Thames, or sit smoking *nargilés* at café tables, beneath the patriarchal plane trees of Emirgan, their branches, draped with the nets of fishermen, spreading generously over an octagonal marble fountain, and a landing-stage guarded by marble lions.

The grandeur of the past still survives along the Bosporus in ample houses, once the homes of Ottoman pashas and merchants; kiosks and palaces built with an elegant European restraint but with a discreet touch of oriental fantasy. Their broad bay windows lean over the water, their glass-fronted doors give on to doorsteps washed by it. Their panelled rooms are thus flooded with its light, their painted ceilings patterned with its reflections, for ever undulating and rippling across their surface. Space is the essence of these rooms, uncrowded with furniture, fitted with divans around the walls, and shallow staircases which curve in a broad double sweep to rooms, as spacious, above. Always there are gardens, shaded by generous trees, rising in tiers up the hillside behind. At Therapia the summer embassies of the European countries survive, some abandoned, some inhabited in season. Here I stayed for a while in the only hotel, once the Tokatlian, lavish with mirrors and the baroque décor of the early twentieth century, where the guests crowded each evening to the plate-glass windows to watch the moon rise from Asia like a giant balloon, throwing a sudden bright light across the water. Built elaborately of wood, the hotel has since been burnt to the ground, like innumerable houses, leaving tell-tale gaps along the waterfront.

My hosts took pleasure in the life of Istanbul, remembering an Ottoman past when it was more refined than today. They had a comfortable motor-launch, and in this we made frequent excursions. Often we went for an all-day picnic to the Marmara, a sea as different from the Bosporus as the Mediterranean from the Atlantic. Between Seraglio Point, with its pile of imperial buildings, and Üsküdar, with its miniature pearl-grey mosque and its earlier mosque, like a Byzantine church, the waters of the Bosporus surge like a whirlpool around the island tower of Leander, then smooth themselves out into the limpid calm of a glittering southern sea. Within the compass of his city the Istanbuli has two, if not three, separate climates. In the past he would have three houses, one in each of them, moving from one to another with the winds. A wind from the North would take him from the city to the shelter of the Marmara, a wind from the South to the cool shores of the Bosporus. Today, despite his limited leisure, the Republican Turk can still do likewise. The penny steamer takes him more speedily than his forebears from one climate to another. Brightening the Marmara coast is a string of popular Riviera resorts, alive with speedboats and sailing craft, their beaches and harbours, their villas and casinos, looking south to the sun amid a pervasive scent of pine-trees. Here we would picnic on the islands of the Princes, once penal settlements for the enemies of emperors and sultans, now places of pleasure for the weekend Turkish crowds, sitting in the cafés to the blare of the radio, strolling and playing and making love in the pine-woods, bathing in secluded sunlit bays. No motor vehicle may land here, and the open horse-drawn victorias, in which the visitors drive, give the flavour of an operette to the scene.

Our picnics were banquets, in the true traditions of Ottoman hospitality, with a variety of *dolmas*, spiced hot and cold dishes and Turkish wines, served by relays of white-coated footmen. My hosts lived in a patriarchal style, with a large household of male retainers —Turkish, Greek, French, Rumanian, Egyptian—who had served them devotedly for years. The palace swarmed with dogs as well. Fortunately it could be divided into two sections, the *haremlik* and the *selamlik*, with doors locked safely between. My hostess loved pekingese, of which she owned a large tribe. But my host had been given a pair of the giant Anatolian sheepdogs which are seldom seen in captivity. They ate a leg of mutton each per day, and would have wolfed the pekingese with delight. Thus a man had to be employed solely to look after these two dogs, keeping them strictly to the *haremlik*, and never for an instant letting them stray from his sight.

It was a harmonious household, with an easy unruffled life. Only occasional dramas disturbed it; but they arose out of very little. One day, in midsummer, an abnormal rainstorm flooded the city and the low-lying land by the Gulf of Izmit, where the railway from Ankara runs. The passengers on the night express, who chanced to include my host returning from a business trip, had to be transferred to a steamer, and were not expected to arrive in Istanbul until late in the evening. This misadventure at once assumed dramatic proportions, throwing the household into a turmoil of anxiety. The boat was several hours late, and by midnight had still not arrived. A mere Nordic family would have left a light on in the hall, and gone to bed; here there was, in any case, a night-watchman to open the door. But this was an oriental family. No one, bar myself, had had an appetite for dinner. Now we sat up, in an atmosphere of tension, drinking countless cups of coffee, telephoning at frequent intervals to know whether the boat had yet arrived.

Eventually, to the intense relief of all, my host appeared. But he brought us news of a further drama. The kennelman, with whom he was travelling, had been seen to board the boat. After it had left, however, there was no sign of him. Had he merely gone ashore again, and missed it? Or had some disaster overtaken him? Had he fallen overboard and been drowned? Could he conceivably and inexplicably have drowned himself deliberately? Deciding that he had merely missed the boat and would come by the next, I crept off, a shamefaced Englishman, to bed. But there was no sleep for the rest of the household. They stayed up hour after hour, drinking coffee, in agonized speculation. Sure enough, next morning, the kennelman appeared, doing a frivolous little caper of welcome as he tripped through the gate. His master and mistress greeted him with tears of laughter and relief. That evening, in exhaustion, tension relieved, they took to their beds before dinner. For days afterwards the drama was recounted, at length and with vivid embroideries, to every guest who came to the house.

Relics of the *ancien régime* still survived in Istanbul, Ottoman princesses who lived on in dignified seclusion, receiving few but their kind, waited upon by Circassian ladies in long pleated dresses who went silently about their business, kissing hands and curtsying at appropriate moments. One of the princesses was a formidable and intelligent old lady, whose standards of taste were so fastidious that she was chronically unable to satisfy them. She was for ever spending her fortune on beautiful houses, then finding them, for some reason or other, uninhabitable. Republicanism seemed bent on thwarting her. In one case a new boulevard was driven through the end of her garden, and she moved out in dudgeon. Seeking greater seclusion, she bought a house, overlooking a secluded cove on the Asiatic shore. No sooner had she decorated and furnished it than the cove was chosen as the anchorage for the presidential yacht, a large vessel which seldom went to sea, and which was now moored permanently before her windows, depriving them of any trace of a view. So she never moved in, and was now living, on a precarious tenure, in a large furnished house in a derelict garden, on the top of a hill commanding the Bosporus. Like our palace, but unlike the houses of modern Turks, it was filled with beautiful objects, brocades and carpets, porcelain and silver, deriving from that elegant fusion of eastern and western taste which the Ottoman Empire achieved. Often, with my hostess, I would drive into Istanbul, combing the shops and bazaars, with varying success, for such treasures. For some years after the Atatürk revolution, when the Turkish aristocracy was selling its possessions, there were plenty to be found. Today they were growing scarcer. In the great covered bazaars there were carpets still; there was Beykoz glass and Turkish silver, delicately and elegantly fashioned. But our happiest hunting-ground was the 'flea-market', a vast and cavernous hangar with innumerable stalls selling the junk of East and West at bargain prices.

Turkish taste at its most sumptuous flourishes in the Topkapi Serai, the palace of the Sultans, crowning the point which dominates the city and all its seas. The Serai is a city in itself, a sequence of spacious squares and gardens adorned with a variety of palaces and kiosks, mosques and cloisters, baths and fountains, treasuries and stables and kitchens. Essentially oriental in style, its buildings combine elaboration of décor with simplicity of design. Exteriors are plain, but for their latticed windows, overhanging eaves and imposing fretted doorways. Interiors are rich with tiles and paintings, carvings and intricate inlays. But the general effect is one of taste rather than grandeur, comfort rather than luxury. The profusion of patterns and colours blends into a harmony of surroundings as restful as a garden of flowers.

The Sultans, moreover, like the Turks of today, sought intimacy. Theirs was the life of the alcove. The suites of rooms where they lived, eating or sleeping in one or another as fancy moved them, are small by palatial standards; and they are comfortable, with low divans around the walls, cupboards and shelves built into the panelling, open grates, with tiled or plastered chimney-pieces, and running water in every room, from a marble basin let into the wall, with an elegant tap. The windows command views over trees and fountains to the shimmering sea below. Throughout the Topkapi Serai there is an air of *douceur de vivre*, belied by the gorier facts of Ottoman history. Only the quarters of the eunuchs, a covered 'prison' of three storeys giving on to a narrow, central courtyard, conveys any suggestion of grimness.

Once, when my hostess was visiting the Serai, a helpful Turkish guide drew her attention to a ceiling, decorated in the rococo style.

'C'était fait,' he said proudly, 'par Monsieur Rococo lui-même.'

The Sultans employed European artists and craftsmen, from the time when Gentile Bellini painted the Conqueror himself. It is the portrait of a grave and dignified figure, mid-way on the walls of the gallery in the Serai between Osman, the first of the Conquerors, with the flaming eyes and flowing beard of the warrior chieftain, and the later, more degenerate despots, with the wary eyes and poker faces of a line of Shylocks. Most curious among the collections of European art are the great services of porcelain, exuberant in style, made for successive sultans of the eighteenth and nineteenth centuries at Sèvres, Vienna, Meissen, Delft, Limoges. They are displayed in the kitchens, with their ranks of towering chimneys, together with huge sets of Celadon and Ming, made to order, but often languishing in their packing-cases until unpacked at the Revolution, and now shown for the first time to the public. As time went on European influence became an influence for the bad. There is a certain shoddiness in the rococo rooms, in the *trompe l'œil* ceilings and elaborate Italian murals. Turkish art is at its best when it remains Turkish in character: a blend of Persian, as in its delicate carvings and tiles, and of Byzantine, as in its rich embroideries and brocades.

As it degenerated it grew more extravagant. It amused my hostess to show me those fabulous works of confectionery, the nineteenth-century palaces of the Sultans, on the Bosporus. Our favourite was Beylerbey, built in the sixties, where the Empress Eugénie stayed, where Abdul Hamid died and where Atatürk entertained King Edward VIII and Mrs. Simpson, on their unofficial but triumphant visit to Istanbul in 1936. Beylerbey resembles a relatively plain white cake, with kiosks on either side of it, like table napkins decoratively folded to a point. Inside, it is a riot of marble, enlivened with sham lapis lazuli columns, and Bohemian glass chandeliers in a galaxy of reds and blues and greens. Each room has a suite of elaborate French furniture in a different design: chairs swirling with ropes or encrusted with shells or, in the bridal suite, fluttering with lovebirds in their nests. In the central hall guests sat beneath standard candelabra, on divans and Gothic gilt chairs, around a fountain as large as a swimming pool.

The Dolmabahçe, built in the fifties, is a wedding-cake, decorating the waterfront: an exuberant fantasy of icing-sugar, half-a-mile in length. Its interminable halls of alabaster and marble and porphyry glitter beneath baroque ceilings, with crystal chandeliers and cut-glass mirrors and chimneypieces of spun Venetian glass. In this incongruous atmosphere Atatürk lived, on occasions, and died. In the throne room, like a grotesque caricature of St. Sophia, his body lay in state before a procession of millions, beneath a chandelier of five hundred lights and a dome flaunting, in *trompe l'œil*, a phantasmagoria of horticultural and architectural *motifs*. Abdul Hamid, already obsessed by the shadow of Revolution, found the palace too exposed for his security. He preferred to conceal himself behind the towering double walls of the park of Yildiz, across the road.

CHAPTER 15

BYZANTIUM (2)

Pera and Stamboul—A Skyline of Domes—St. Sophia and its Professor—Other Byzantine Churches—The Golden Gates —The Mosques of Sinan—The Sweet Waters of Europe

ISTANBUL is in effect two cities, divided by the Golden Horn. One is Pera, now Beyoğlu, the ill-planned jangling city of the Europeans; the other is Stamboul, the more spacious city of Byzantium, with its incomparable skyline of mosques. Pera is a nineteenth-century quarter, with narrow canyons of cobbled lanes careering headlong down to the water. Its ponderous tenements, gaping obscenely, ring with the clangour of trams and the grinding of gears, as the traffic hurries irritably upwards and downwards through precipitous winding streets. Until horns were forbidden it was a pandemonium of noise; now this is replaced by a tattoo, as the drivers, rather than run down the crowds, beat with their hands on the sides of their vehicles. The long narrow rue de Pera, the most ignoble of international streets, bustles all day long with office crowds, swarming into the milk bars and the sausage shops and the shoeshine parlours which now supplement, in the German-American manner, the more sedate Turkish cafés of the past. From the top of it a new city of modern apartment blocks and streamlined public buildings spreads out over the hillsides, beyond the spacious Taksim gardens, its well-planned boulevards curving downwards to the Bosporus below.

From the sombre warehouses and quays of Galata, with their murky cafés, the Galata bridge floats low over the Golden Horn, through a forest of masts and sails and funnels from the shipping packed close in the harbour. By the bridgehead the Valide mosque, with its pyramid of domes and its minarets, like lighthouses, commands the approach to the Moslem city with a calm and spacious dignity.

The skyline of Istanbul is still inherently that of Byzantium.

Eliminate the pencilled minarets and it becomes a city of domes, looking much as it might have done had the Byzantine Empire survived for another few centuries. Ottoman architecture is no mere imitation of the Byzantine. It derives from additional influences, notably the Persian and the Arabic, and is essentially different in plan from the Christian. Moreover what the Turks borrowed from others they transformed into something essentially Turkish. But in Constantinople the first mosque to be built after the conquest was designed by a Greek architect, and was undoubtedly inspired by the system of vaulting used in St. Sophia, with its half-domes extending and supporting the main dome. 'It may be', suggests Mr. Spencer Corbett, 'that Mohamet II liked the great open area of floor in Aghia Sophia, found it well suited for Moslem use when the church had been turned into a mosque, and ordered Christodulos, his Greek architect, to provide similar advantages in the mosque which he was building to celebrate the victory of Islam.'[1] The Byzantine Empire in its decline lacked the resources to develop this style, which therefore lapsed for nearly a thousand years until the Turks took it over. Thus St. Sophia, with its majestic buttressed dome, stands as the prototype of the mosques which crown the ridge, like a series of rounded summits, between the Golden Horn and the Marmara.

St. Sophia owes much to an American, Professor Whittemore, who became, as it were, its familiar spirit. Through his friendship with Atatürk he ensured its maintenance as a museum, and devoted some twenty years of his life to uncovering its mosaics. The Professor was a slow-moving sprite with a deep, sonorous voice and a skin as pale and as crinkled as tissue-paper, who lived in imagination in the Byzantine Age. In fact he lived in a house on the Bosporus with an old friend, also an American, whom he had known since schooldays, and whom he teased unmercifully, arousing angry protests and an unwavering devotion.

It was the Professor who took me to stand, for the first time, beneath the dome of St. Sophia. Its serene expanse, together with the immaculate symmetry of the colonnades around us, absorbed the profuse decoration of the sculpture and the marbles to achieve a masterpiece of grandiose simplicity. Here, embodying treasures of pagan architecture from temples throughout the classical world—from Rome, from Athens, from Delphi, from Ephesus, from Baalbek—is the

[1] *Architectural Review*. London: May 1953.

apotheosis of classical art, given a new illumination and a new continuity by its translation into Christian terms. We stood for a few moments in silence. Then the Professor intoned, with a broad sweep of the arm:

'*It's volu-metric.*'

The jargon did not offend, for it expressed the essence of St. Sophia, a work of art conceived in terms of volume, not merely of geometry, emulating the skies with its vault, not merely enclosing them, like the other lesser mosques. When Justinian first saw it completed by his two architects from Miletus and Tralles, he exclaimed: 'Glory be to God, who has thought me worthy of accomplishing such a work. Oh Solomon, I have conquered you.' His emotions may well have been shared by Fatih (Mohamet II) the enlightened conqueror of Byzantium, who ordered its preservation, together with all the mosaics, and maintained its continuity of worship as a mosque. The mosaics survived until the nineteenth century, when they were covered over with plaster, and with an inferior decoration in the arabesque style. Professor Whittemore had uncovered all that survive, and was now expounding to me, with fervour, their peculiar '*con*-ceptual' quality, as opposed to the mere '*per*-ceptual' creations of the Latins.

'You do not *see* the figure of Christ. You *react* to Him.'

The Pantocrator, who filled the Dome until a century ago, has disappeared. But other images of Christ have been revealed once more. He sits above the southern door, an alert Greek child on the lap of the Virgin, flanked by the Emperors Justinian and Constantine. It is a group conceived in an advancing perspective, as though moving forward to meet the World.

'You do not look at the Virgin,' the Professor whispered slowly. '*She* looks at *you*.'

She looks out also from above the altar, a long slim seated figure, all robed in black, with the slim child on her lap—a pair at once human and Divine whom the Angel Gabriel, in resplendent white with enfolding wings, protects. The mature Christ, bearded and grave in demeanour, presides over a gallery with the Virgin on one hand and a mournful John the Baptist, clad in green, head bowed, on the other—figures achieving in mosaic the refinement and depth of painting.

This was the gallery designed for the ladies of the court of Theodora, whose praises the Professor was now chanting: 'A woman as great as the dome . . . as great as the Law . . . as great as Belisarius.'

But now he must take me away to luncheon. It was a mistake to see too much at a time. We walked down the hill, past the Sublime Porte, and through the bustling market by the Golden Horn, a place soaked in the smell of the sea and its produce. The stalls were adorned with large round trays, painted a brilliant scarlet and gleaming with silver fishes, arranged in a decorative pattern. Others were piled with pyramids of eggs and lined with cages, where chickens languished, awaiting sale and slaughter. Farther along the narrow musty street were the booths of the broom-makers and basket-workers, where small boys deftly caned the seats of chairs. Here was a Greek restaurant, a crowded chop-house with sawdust on the floor, where peasants jostled ministers and Ambassadors and merchants, and the grey-moustached proprietor, Pandeli, presided at a counter, distributing gargantuan helpings and shouting ribald commands to waiters and customers alike. Pandeli's takings at midday were such that he could afford to close the restaurant and gamble them happily away each evening.

I knew that the Professor's appetites were frugal, for I had seen him by St. Sophia in the luncheon hour, sitting on the edge of a fountain, taking a lump of bread and some olives from his pocket, nibbling at an olive and throwing the bread to the birds. Thus I was hardly surprised to see, placed before us, not one of Pandeli's famous mixed grills, but a modest portion of steamed fish, divided into two. There was at first nothing to drink. But when we had eaten half our fish, the Professor recollected himself, called for the waiter, and consulted him earnestly over the wine list. Presently the waiter reappeared with a bottle. The Professor took a taste, and nodded with approval. The waiter poured us out two glasses of an excellent brand of water.

Afterwards the Professor led me to the Museum of Antiquities, pausing to marvel, in its garden, before two vast purple sarcophagi, built of imperial porphyry and adorned only with the Cross, in which Byzantine emperors lie buried. Scorning classical masterpieces, he then hurried me through the Alexandrine to the Byzantine rooms. Here we wandered for an hour, amid Christian reliefs and fragments of columns, admiring a delicate capital of windblown acanthus, and another of bearded heads with acanthus leaves for hair. Finally we came to a small Byzantine pulpit, built of green porphyry, austerely simple, yet a living piece of sculpture. The Professor stood for a long time before it, in silence. Then he murmured:

'It *looks* at you. It advances towards you, like . . . like . . . like a *tank!*'

* * *

After he had uncovered the mosaics of St. Sophia, Professor Whittemore started to restore those of the Kahriye Jami, the Byzantine church of St. Saviour in Chora. The work was continued after his death by his successor, Dr. Underwood. On a later visit to Istanbul I saw it nearing its end. Under his direction a group of keen young men, for the most part Christians of European origin, sat perched on a scaffolding, working away with sponges and brushes and pincers, piecing fragments of mosaic together. Thanks to the scaffolding it was possible, for a little longer, to see the mosaics at close range; soon it would go, and they would retire into a remoter perspective. Here is little of the solemnity of the mosaics of St. Sophia, but a series of gay human scenes, some centuries later in date, illustrating the life of Christ and of the Virgin. The artists have enjoyed portraying life as they saw it lived around them. The Virgin riding to Bethlehem is a Greek peasant woman on her donkey. The figure of Joseph, bending over the Child in Mary's arms, is that of any Greek father of a family. The Child, in a series of intimate domestic scenes, rides to Nazareth on his father's shoulder; learns to walk, taking his first seven steps; plays among animals and flowers, in a springlike peasant landscape. Other children scramble around the rich man's table, picking up crumbs as in a game. The marriage at Cana is a Greek peasant feast, with inviting loaves, and wine poured from pots like those of today.

Work had barely been begun on the Fethiye Mosque, the Church of St. Mary Pammakaristos, perhaps the last of the churches whose mosaics and frescoes are to be redeemed. I found it with difficulty. Built of a soft pink stone, with courses of brick, it languishes in a remote neglected quarter of the city, its battered walls rising high above the roofs of the mean houses which cluster around it. Its windows had gone, and it had been occupied on a large scale by pigeons, soiling its walls and its pavements with their débris. They were abetted by the janitor, an aged red-head in a fur-collared coat, who zealously fed them, together with his hens and his goat. Only the Pantocrator emerged unimpaired from a dome torn with holes and pitted with the nests of the birds.

Sultan Fatih, the conqueror of Constantinople, was an enlightened monarch. After the initial massacre, less grave than that of the Crusades, which followed his capture of the city in 1453, he proclaimed himself protector of the Greek Church, appointed a Patriarch, and gave orders that the churches should be preserved, whether for Christian or—more commonly—for Moslem worship. Thus some two dozen Byzantine churches survive, in some form or another, in Istanbul today. I spent several days exploring those which are not entirely in ruins, making long journeys by tram to the ends of the city, where it peters out into shacks and cabbage patches, losing myself in warrens of cobbled slum streets as I searched for the rough weathered walls and the compressed fluted domes, which distinguish the churches at sight from the smooth faced leaden-domed mosques. My favourite among them was St. Sergius and St. Bacchus, known as Little St. Sophia, since it resembles a replica of the cathedral in miniature. It is a neglected building, down by the railway, with the Marmara shimmering just beyond. Its courtyard has degenerated into a farmyard, with chickens pecking amid the refuse of the city, and pigeons fluttering around the roofs with a sound like laundry on a clothes line, flapping intermittently in the breeze. Within its square of walls it is little more than a tall octagonal colonnade, rising to the dome in two storeys, but of spacious proportions, with columns of fine coloured marbles, and capitals of a delicate basket tracery.

The largest of these churches is that of the Pantocrator. Its plain walls, broken only by long rounded niches, stand out like bastions from the ridge of old Stamboul. It is in fact two complete churches—if not three, since the two, with their long vaulted aisles, are joined by the funeral chapel of the Paleologues, with the ruins of a monastery around it. Like other Byzantine churches, it was looted by the Latins during their occupation of the city, and some of its treasures removed to St. Mark's at Venice. Inside nothing remains but its unmistakable Byzantine form. Outside the tomb of its founder, the Empress Irene, still proclaims the Cross, carved on its green marble slabs, now lying broken and abandoned beneath a dilapidated canopy in the midst of a dump of refuse.

At the foot of the ridge, by the banks of the Golden Horn, the walls of St. Theodosius (the Gül Jami or Mosque of the Roses) rise as high and austere as those of the warehouses and workshops crowding around it. Beneath the spacious vaults of this church the Emperor Constantine, with his patriarch and his senate and a large crowd of his subjects, worshipped for the last time, throughout the night before the fall of the city, to be slaughtered or captured by the Turks in the morning. One tradition states that the Emperor was buried here. More likely his body was never found, despite the orders of the Sultan to search for it. The Kilise Jami, perhaps the monastic church of St. Theodore, is a rose-coloured building, hidden amid winding streets. The marble Crosses in the walls are undefaced, the Corinthian columns still stand, the corrugated roofs have been repaired and the mosaics restored through the gift of a Moslem patron. In a far corner of the city is the Church of St. Andrew, to whom tradition attributes the first Christian community of Byzantium. In use as the mosque of the quarter, its Crosses have been defaced, and some of its Byzantine columns have been painted a sacred green. Intimate in atmosphere, it stands amid planes and cypresses, confronted by an ancient dead tree with a decaying latticed building around it, surrounded by a 'village' of grey wooden houses shaded by trellises of vines.

But of all the relics of Byzantium the most evocative is the Stoudion, once the city's chief monastery, dedicated to John the Baptist, where a thousand monks, in relays of three choirs, sang day and night in a perpetual service to the glory of God. The Crusaders destroyed it; the Paleologues restored it; the son of a Sultan, converted to Christianity, was buried in it; fires and earthquakes finally reduced it to ruins. It is a Hellenistic basilica, one of two which survive in the city. Facing the Sea of Marmara, it stands in a neglected garden among trees festooned with ivy. In its forecourt a devoted janitor lives in a shack, smoking his *nargilé* beneath aged pistachio trees by the side of a crumbling fountain. He unlocks the door into the nave, as it once was, and there, open to the skies, within jagged walls, a row of Corinthian columns strides down towards the Marmara, with a frieze above it, and beneath it, stretching over a wide expanse of floor, a mosaic of coloured marbles. The marble is splintering off the columns and the walls; the mosaic is disintegrating, its pieces scattered over the dusty ground like those of an unfinished jigsaw puzzle. But the Stoudion, in its majestic decay and seclusion, still has the flavour of Byzantium, and of the classical age before it.

From here Constantinople ebbs away to its golden walls. A fortress, just within them, guards the approach to the city. It is the castle of the Seven Towers, four of them Byzantine, three of them Turkish, a fearsome prison where the Sultans imprisoned their enemies and where once even a Sultan himself was imprisoned. Here, beneath the Tower of the Ambassadors, are dark insalubrious dungeons, where foreigners languished and raged and died: diplomats, merchants, captains of ships, who have left inscriptions on the walls, in Greek, in Latin, in German, in French, recording their miseries. From its overgrown courtyard the Golden Gate, the Arc de Triomphe of the early Byzantine Emperors, leads out into the open fields and orchards of Thrace. Its central arch is now blocked and an adjoining gateway serves the city in its place. The gate's rectangular marble bastions, weathered today more silver than gold, still tower before the city, in all their massive simplicity, with a triumphant imperial air. On the one hand they are lapped by the waves of the Marmara; on the other the walls still march, in an unbroken procession of towers, far into the distance towards the shores of the Golden Horn.

Fatih the Conqueror was buried, and his mosque was built, on the site of the patriarchal Church of the Holy Apostles, near the head of the aqueduct which Valens built, and which still stretches, in two storeys of arches, across the Atatürk Boulevard. Built originally by a Greek, in a style still close to the Christian, it is a large but simple building, contrasting with the grander, more imposing mosques of later centuries. Like them, it stands amid the buildings of the welfare state which flourished in Turkey from the Middle Ages onwards: a hospital, a library, a soup kitchen, a bath-house, and a series of schools with walls like a fortress around it. To reach the mosque I had to weave my way through the sheep-market, like that of any country town, which huddles around its walls. Amid the bleating a young Turkish woman knelt by the Conqueror's tomb, talking away to him quietly, as though in intimate conversation. Equally simple in its style, more rustic still in its surroundings is the Selim Mosque, rising amid cypresses from the far end of the ridge, near the Edirne Gate. Reached by a rough road, by the edge of a large walled depression where orchards and allotments and unkempt gardens have grown up from the bed of a Byzantine cistern, it has a secluded white courtyard, and a tomb where Selim I lies buried amid an elegant décor of tiles, in springlike greens and yellows. A Turkish epitaph compared his reign to the 'afternoon sun which, though it casteth long shadows, is but fleeting'.

The Ottoman sun came to its zenith in the sixteenth century, with the succeeding reign of Suleiman the Magnificent. Appropriately, it produced a great architect, Mirmar Sinan. He, above all others, transformed the Greek city of Byzantium into the Turkish city of Istanbul. Sinan, paradoxically—or perhaps characteristically—was no Turk. His parents may have been Greek, or Armenian or even Bosnian. He was a Janissary, who served as a military engineer both on the Persian and European fronts, and who won a reputation for his skill as a bridge-builder. Suleiman employed him to build palaces and mosques instead. Employing a large staff of assistants, he built, between the age of fifty and eighty-nine when he died, one hundred and thirty-one mosques, nineteen tombs, sixty-two schools, thirty-three palaces, a similar number of Turkish baths, and fifty-six other buildings, including hospitals, aqueducts and bridges—a total of three hundred and forty-four buildings, which Evliya, such was his fame, magnified to three thousand and sixty. His influence extended even to India, where one of his pupils designed Akbar's palaces in Lahore, Delhi and Agra.[1] The Ottoman Turks were a military people, and it is thus fitting that their great mosques should be the work of an architect whose primary gifts were order in design, accuracy in method, and competence in construction. As an engineer Sinan did not always attain, in his mosques, to the inspiration inherent in either the Persian mosques or the Greek and Roman churches. He was a down-to-earth architect, sober in his aspirations. But as such he has dignified the skyline of Istanbul with buildings, at once massive as fortresses, logical as pyramids and light as balloons, which, inspired as they may initially have been by the Byzantines, nevertheless rank with assurance as works of art, distinctively and proudly Turkish.

The essentials of Sinan's mosques are the dome and the minaret, the colonnade and the courtyard. The dome proliferates into an attendant sequence of half-domes and 'domelets', all smoothly clothed in lead. The minarets taper upwards to flank and protect them. The courtyard is spacious, and usually clear but for a single polygonal fountain, similarly capped with lead. The colonnade surrounds it; domed vaults resting on a progression of slender columns, with stalactite capitals and pointed arches. Decoration is restrained, as in any functional building; proportions are as flawless as a proposition of Euclid. The interior is a broad open space, lit by tiers of windows, its arcades not confining the centre of worship, like those of St. Sophia, but opening it out, in a series of perspectives of vaults and arches. Only the interior decoration,

[1] For this and other information on Sinan I am indebted to the article by Mr. Spencer Corbett in the *Architectural Review. op. cit.*

generally crude with the designs and the colours of a later date, detracts from the dignity of the whole. For ever creating variations on a single central theme, Sinan's mosques differ essentially from one another only as the architect himself developed in age and skill and lucidity: the Suleimanieh, for example, improving on the Sultan Ahmed, as art improves on geometry, until his masterpiece is achieved, at the age of eighty-five, in the Selimieh at Edirne.

Istanbul still reflects, to a great extent, the sixteenth and seventeenth centuries. Along the tram-lines of today Sinan's influence survives in good-mannered buildings: colleges, libraries, *hans* and tombs, above all fountains at once graceful and functional. For all its modern congestion, the city has an atmosphere of space. Everywhere trees grow freely, planes and magnolias spreading generous unpollarded branches across gardens and courts and graveyards. And from everywhere, framed by the trees and the minarets, there is a sudden fresh view of the sea, sealing, as it were, the union of art and nature, of land and water.

Beyond the walls, by the Sweet Waters of Europe—now alas! soured by the refuse from factories and wharves—is the rickety village and rambling mosque of Eyub. It is a village of cafés and eating-shops, a mosque whose precincts are alive with the soothing hubbub of birds. Pigeons have converted the walls into dovecotes. Storks and herons nest on the roofs and in the trees. Cats prowl through the court-yards, tended and fed by village women. An old man lives in an ancient plane tree, with a door in its vast hollow trunk. Villagers and suppliants come here to feed the birds and give alms to the beggars and pay their respects to a companion of the Prophet, who died fighting the Greeks beneath the walls of Constantinople. His mortal remains lie in a tomb like a lofty drawing-room, raised for him by Fatih the Conqueror, a pattern of tiles covering its walls and the external walls of his mosque around it.

Behind the mosque and the village I walked up a path through overgrown cemeteries, where nightingales sing, and where generations of Istanbulis lie buried, their tombstones fashioned into the likeness of turbans or carved with sprays of flowers. At the top of the hill I sat down in a café, where Pierre Loti used to sit, watching the sunset. The proprietor showed me a faded photograph of Loti, whom he claimed to remember. The view down the Golden Horn, with its metallic blue sheet of water and the curve of the ridge with its architectural summits, was as still and distinct as an image in some *camera obscura*. Presently, sure enough, as the sun sank behind us, the set piece materialized, and the windows of Istanbul became a thousand pinpoints of liquid flaming light. The Golden Horn had indeed turned to gold.

CHAPTER 16

BITHYNIA AND THRACE

Bursa—Blue Streets and Green Orchards—Ottoman Mosques and Tombs—Mysian Olympus—A Byzantine Bath—Nicaea and its Walls—Adrianople and Greece

THE PEOPLE OF ISTANBUL travel by sea without fuss. Once or twice during the summer we would drive down after breakfast to Galata, put a car on the boat, and sail away across the Marmara leaving behind us the austere imperial barracks and the ornate modern railway station of Haydar Paşa, making for the port of Mudanya, on the Bithynian shore. For three hours the Turkish passengers sat stolidly on their rows of seats, as in a bus or a tram, talking a little, reading newspapers, or gazing in silence out to sea. At Mudanya the car was soon off the boat, and we were driving up over the hillside, in comfortable time for a good luncheon at Bursa. The boat had translated us as it were from the North to the Mediterranean, from the glassy clarity of the shores of the Bosporus into a landscape soft with vines and olives and distant smoky hills. From the verandah of the Çelik Palas Otel we looked down over a plain as prolific as Lombardy, with armies of poplars marching across it, from the foothills of snow-capped Olympus to a sun-dried range beyond.

Bursa was the capital of Prusias, King of Bithynia and friend of Hannibal; then the Prusa of the Romans, where Pliny served as Governor; finally the Bursa where the Ottoman Turks made their capital in the early days of their Empire. Built on the slopes of Mysian Olympus, it luxuriates amid a wealth of trees and gardens, fed by the generous streams of the mountain. The colour of its landscape inspires colour in its buildings. From a spur above the city I looked down into streets and courtyards flooded with blue. The Turks of Bursa wash their houses in many colours—ochre or pink or tomato or chocolate—but mainly in this cerulean blue, creating the illusion that the sky has been poured into the town, making rivers and pools of it beneath the russet tiled roofs and their attendant spreading trees. At sundown, when the sky paled, Bursa still glowed blue, as though it had greedily drained the last vestige of colour away from it.

I wandered down into the bazaars, where the cobbled streets were roofed with vines, or arched with the boughs of giant plane trees, each sheltering a cluster of stalls piled brightly with fruits and vegetables, spices and herbs. No Turk here will cut down a tree. If a tree meets a street, then the street gives way, politely bowing around and away from it and thus giving to Bursa a wayward informal air. Silk is the pride of its bazaars, fed by the mulberries of Olympus, woven century after century by Bursa families on a multitude of looms, throbbing away throughout the town, often in timbered shanties of a Dickensian age and decrepitude. The merchants assemble in cloistered *hans*, as large as college quadrangles, their gateways still grand in decay. The Feast of Bayram was approaching, and the butchers had decorated their carcases of meat with golden spangles, placing a ruff of coloured paper around a headless neck and a single flower by an orifice. The streets had become pens for flocks of Bayram sheep, munching away at their clover, arrayed in bead necklaces, with bows in their tails, their coats dipped pink and yellow and brown and green with an air of fantasy appropriate to the Feast. As I watched, a gentleman in a city suit paid over his money, hoisted a pink ram on to his shoulders, and bore it away in a cab.

Above the blue streets and the gardens and the orchards of Bursa the mosques and tombs arise, their architectural forms reflecting the forms of nature around them. Their minarets match the cypresses, their blue leaded domes the leaf-green domes of the fruit-trees. As Fatih, the conqueror of Constantinople, employed a Greek to build his mosque, so Murad I, the builder of Bursa, employed a Latin—an Italian architect, captured in a neighbouring battle. But the decorative influences on the mosques of Bursa are Persian. Simple in form, they flower internally with tiles and sculpture: gardens within themselves, now that the Ottoman Turks have descended from the austerity of the plateau to the sensuous ease of the coastal valleys.

This early Ottoman style, at once simpler and more refined than Sinan's, blossomed a century before him with the Green Mosque, and the Green Tomb of Mohamet I at its side. The tiles covering its walls are severe enough: plain hexagons of a dark luminous green. But in the prayer *niche* geometry has burst into bloom, putting forth leaves and flowers within a framework of stalactites and flowing Islamic calligraphy. The outer doorway gives similar ornament to the austere front of the mosque. The galleries and chambers, surrounding the place of prayer, are encrusted with plasterwork as rich as embroidery. The tomb of the Sultan is an octagonal building, a beacon of clashing blues and greens, flanked by sentinel cypresses and shining to all quarters of the town. Outside, the tiles which cover the walls are modern, from Kutahya, and plain in design. Inside they are of an earlier period, from Iznik, where a Genoese factory copied Persian designs for the Sultans. They are said to have been designed by a Persian artist from Tabriz. Profuse in their floral decoration, they have in their colouring little of the red which adorned the later, more essentially Turkish, tiles of Kutahya, with their elegant carnation and tulip designs. Here the flowers are the yellow crocus and a species of daisy in a variety of blues and greens.

'Seventy-seven varieties,' my guide assured me. He was given to statistics. An accomplished *Muezzin*, he claimed to know six hundred pages of the Koran (at fifteen lines to a page) by heart. Each morning, to keep his voice in training, he sang forty pages of it before breakfast to his wife. Straight from the throat, he began to try it out on me. But I hurriedly interrupted him. We had the mosques of other Sultans to visit. I lingered in all of them, enjoying the sobriety of their architecture and the grace of their décor; content to relax by the hour in the calm of their courtyards, the refreshment of their fountains, the shade of their trees; finding company moreover in the cafés beside them, their vine-covered terraces looking down over the blue streets to the deep green plain below.

The earliest and largest of the mosques is the Ulu Jami, an imposing barrack of a building, with a profusion of domes, commanding the central square of the town. Originally, like most Ottoman mosques of the fourteenth century, it was built without minarets. Now two of them rise at the corners, later additions to the building. As large as a Seljuk mosque, I found it filled with people, washing and praying. They washed barefoot at a series of taps, by a polygonal marble fountain inhabited by goldfish, the water brimming over from it into a channel cut in the stone at its foot. They prayed with their caps back to front and their foreheads to the ground, civilians and soldiers, old and young. A small boy sat on a camp stool, swaying from side to side as he read the Koran, with his face towards Mecca; another squatted beside him, chanting in a high childish voice. Outside in the courtyard, beneath the plane trees, pedlars sold Arabic texts and beads and bottles of scent. In every direction there was something to please the eye: a fountain beneath a carved wooden canopy, with a wooden pumpkin dome; a pointed doorway, in the Persian manner; an iron-work railing with a delicate Gothic pattern—all products of the crafts-men whom the Ottoman Court gathered around it in every age.

Osman, who captured Bursa, was no more than an Emir, like the rulers of other small Turkish states in Asia Minor. It was his son Orhan who converted the emirate into an empire, by driving the Greeks out of Asia and gaining a foothold in Europe. He did so largely by backing one Byzantine faction against another, an intrigue which involved his marriage with Theodora, the daughter of the Byzantine Emperor Cantacuzene. Her father, quoted by Gibbon, 'describes, with shameful satisfaction, the dishonour of the purple' in the imperial camp. 'At a signal the curtains were suddenly withdrawn, to disclose the bride, or the victim, encircled by kneeling eunuchs and hymenaeal torches: the sound of flutes and trumpets proclaimed the joyful event; and her pretended happiness was the theme of the nuptial song, which was chanted by such poets as the age could produce.'[1] But she was allowed to remain a Christian, in the Harem. My Turkish guide pointed out to me a tomb, which he declared to be hers, among the tombs of twenty-one of Orhan's dependents. An old black crow of a woman was stroking the brocaded covering of the sarcophagus, then stroking her own face, before hobbling away in the direction of the hospital, with a bearded husband clad in the thick black tweeds of Mount Olympus.

The essential flavour of Bursa pervades the graveyard of these first Ottoman Sultans and their children. Reverting in death to the early austerity of their race, they lie in a honey-sweet rose-garden on the slopes of Olympus in octagonal walled tombs of a severe design, devoid of ornament. Following the example of Murad II, who desired that his place of burial should be exposed, like that of a poor man, to rain and snow, their graves are of bare earth, watered in season through openings in the domes which surmount them, and thus in spring giving life to indoor lawns of fresh green grass. Around each grave is a plain colonnade, perhaps with Byzantine capitals, on a paved stone floor,

[1] *The Decline and Fall of the Roman Empire*. Chapter VI.

while the walls are of undecorated, hexagonal tiles, in pure deep Persian blues. Similar tiles cover the façade of the mosque of Murad, and the walls of a *medresse*, with vaults of brick, which adjoin the garden. Nearby is a modest half-timbered house, which the Turks have restored with tiles and panelling and zigzag brickwork, as the birthplace of Fatih the Conqueror himself.

Mysian Olympus, which dominates Bursa and its plain, is a humane and accessible throne with ample room for both gods and men. We drove slowly up it, across meadows of harebell and yarrow and thyme, through forests of chestnut and beech, then of juniper and pine, up into the purer air, beyond the tree line, where the snow lay thinly over the Alpine pastures. Here is a large but haphazard hotel, where we lunched amid a steaming crowd of Turkish winter sportsmen. Above us the mountain coiled on lazily, like a benevolent monster, towards its grey elephantine summit. A smooth peak of marble, it can be climbed without effort. But we preferred to walk out over one of its shoulders, to a spur which falls, with dramatic suddenness, down to the plain below. We took our time, relishing the scents, first of the snow-clad meadows, then of the pine-forest, warmed by a sun which shone from an unclouded sky. A white vulture planed lazily over our head, like a malevolent god. But as we emerged into the open the sky clouded abruptly, and an angry storm broke over us, enveloping the mountain in Olympian torrents of rain. Finding no shelter, we could only walk back through it, sliding along paths which were now rivers of red mud, saturated to our skins as though by some aquatic prank of the gods. I dried my clothes in the hotel kitchen, amid smells of *kebabs* grilling on skewers and *dolmas* steaming in olive oil, warming myself as I did so with acrid draughts of *raki*. On returning to Bursa I plunged straight into the hot sulphurous waters of the indoor swimming-pool attached to the hotel, lazily splashing and soaking and after an hour relaxing beneath the hands of an accomplished masseur. Here was ample compensation for the caprices of Olympus.

Bursa, throughout the centuries, has been renowned for its baths, flowing from the hot and cold springs of the mountain. Pliny, as governor of Bithynia, asked and obtained leave from Trajan to repair an ancient and ruinous bath, 'a work which the dignity of the city and the splendour of your reign seems to demand'. It would have the advantage, he added, of 'ornamenting the city in a part which is at present exceedingly deformed, and actually make it more spacious without pulling down any buildings, but merely by advantageously opening out the ruins time has made'.[1] In the Turkish baths the large number of naked people reminded Dallaway of the day of the Resurrection, 'since the sources of water in which they bathe have no other origin than the fountains of Paradise'. Today the baths of Bursa, with their broad tiled domes, their marble floors and slabs and fountains gushing with hot or cold water, are still as numerous and as elegant as its mosques. The oldest is at Çekirge, a suburb of Bursa which has become a holiday resort. It was built in the time of Justinian, and with its weathered walls and fluted domes has the aspect of a Byzantine church. The Turks have added an outer hall, its fretted woodwork painted a pale pink and grey, where the bathers recline on bunks amid piles of coloured towels, while a fountain cools water-melons and mineral-waters for their refreshment.

Within are two domed chambers, wholly Byzantine in style, both panelled and paved with marble. In the first the basin of a fountain, shaped into petals like those of a flower, flows over a broad fluted pedestal. In the second, a round sunken pool steams gently, set within a round colonnade whose columns have acanthus and basket capitals, like those of St. Sophia itself. The four corners are fashioned into vaulted alcoves with marble basins finely moulded. A marble tap, in the shape of a porpoise, pours water into the bath over a stretch of mosaic pavement. Sitting half submerged on the marble steps, slowly acclimatizing my body to the heat of the clouded water, I watched the bathers wallowing with their heads just above it, washing their bodies and massaging those of their companions, as bathers had done in this pool, beneath this dome and within these columns, for one thousand five hundred years. Nor can its atmosphere have differed greatly from that of the Roman bath, which Pliny built to the honour and glory of Trajan.

* * *

As we left Bursa, early in the morning, the cypresses and the minarets stood out in isolation above a mist which smoked gently in the folds of the foothills. We drove eastwards along the valley, prolific with mulberries and walnuts, maize and tobacco, which hung drying on the walls of the houses in swags and garlands, like some baroque architectural motif; then up and across the plateau through fields of

[1] *Letters from Bithynia.* X.

sunflowers, like fields of girls, standing openfaced and expectant, or drooping with downcast faces and tousled locks. Presently the long blue Lake of Iznik lay beneath us like a trough between the mountains, with the ruined city of Nicaea placed strategically at the head of it.

We sat drinking coffee in its village, doves crooning in the branches of the lime trees above us, while storks, dangling ungainly pink legs, took off clumsily from the nests with which they had encumbered the moss-grown roofs. We found a Seljuk mosque, but no longer a Christian church, since it was destroyed, with its precious Byzantine mosaics, at the time of the expulsion of the Greeks in the nineteen-twenties. Little remains of the great classical and Byzantine city but an expanse of fields and gardens, scattered with ruins, and enclosed still within a formidable enceinte of double fortress walls. Built by the Romans of stone, by the Byzantines of brick, they glow pink in the sunlight, by the blue waters of the lake, their dignity enhanced by imposing gateways and an array of massive rounded towers. Within them we found relics perhaps of a hippodrome, and of a tomb beneath it, plastered in sinister fashion with an amalgam of mud and human bones. My hostess liked to think that they were the bones of early Christians, devoured in the arena by lions.

We drove westwards once more along the shores of the lake, its surface eddying with concentric whorls and circles of water. The mountains swept up from it, their groves of olives encroaching, like clouds of blue smoke, on young green beech forests, marching up to the skyline. Covered ox-wagons, laden with red peppers and melons, lumbered along the dusty roads to the market, while peasants by the roadside, sitting cross-legged on sledges, threshed their crops of grain. We reached Yalova, relaxing in a spa hotel amid hot springs and luxuriant gardens. After dark we took the ferry across the Gulf of Izmit, and thence home to the lights of Istanbul.

* * *

The train into Europe, from Istanbul, runs along the edge of the Marmara, from the station where the walls of Constantine's palace once stood. One night it took me, on the last lap of my journey to Adrianople: a journey which had brought me in space from the borders of Syria to the borders of Bulgaria and Greece, in time from the Alexandrine through the Roman and Byzantine to the Ottoman Age, with excursions into the earlier ages of the Greeks. It was a worthy outpost of Asia in Europe which met my eyes across the Thracian fields, next morning. There, billowing up from the plain, beyond the banks of the broad Maritza River, was Sinan's masterpiece, the mosque of Selim II. With a soaring ease the single voluminous dome rises from eight solid piers. That is all: as his life draws to an end, the architect has attained to the ultimate simplicity. Chishull describes the Selimieh as 'like a theatre, consisting of one stately room'. Elegant arcades surround it. Tiled panels, with bold floral designs, adorn it. Windows fill it with light from above. The delicacy of its ornament balances the manliness of its style. Colour illuminates it, not only within but without, where alternate courses of red and gold stone grace the delicate arches of its cloisters. Strength is implicit in its massive buttresses, dignity in its guardian minarets, standing at each of the four corners, and its satellite pinnacles, like minarets in miniature, flanking the impassive leaden dome.

Adrianople, like Bursa, was once a capital of the Ottoman Empire. Today, as Edirne, it is merely a prosperous country town. Relics of its former grandeur survive in other mosques, and a *han*, and a caravanserai. But the Selimieh was all I wanted. I walked back to the railway station, and waited for my train, to the unfamiliar sounds of Greek music from a gramophone. The train came in from the Bulgarian frontier: a single empty carriage, marked Svilengrad–Istanbul. Turkish carriages were coupled to it, and we set off, eccentrically, through a section of Greece which cuts across the line to the Maritza, below Edirne. Greek trains stop at its stations, Turkish trains do not. Greek gendarmes singing Greek songs, talking in their quicker, crisper language, accompanied us across it. Greek peasants, later than the Turks with their harvest, were bringing it home in long blue carts. Their villages were shabbier than the Turkish villages, with straw-roofed huts and large plain churches. Their roads were mere tracks. But they were welcoming, lively. Back across the Maritza, in Turkish territory, we stopped at the frontier station of Uzun Köpru. A train was standing at the platform, marked Istanbul–Salonika. It was like a signpost pointing to Greece.

Edinburgh—London

1954–1955

INDEX